Eastern Europe 1237–42

COMBAT

Mongol Warrior
VERSUS
European Knight

Stephen Turnbull

Illustrated by Giuseppe Rava

OSPREY PUBLISHING

Bloomsbury Publishing Plc

Kemp House, Chawley Park, Cumnor Hill, Oxford OX2 9PH, UK

29 Earlsfort Terrace, Dublin 2, Ireland

1385 Broadway, 5th Floor, New York, NY 10018, USA

E-mail: info@ospreypublishing.com

www.ospreypublishing.com

OSPREY is a trademark of Osprey Publishing Ltd

First published in Great Britain in 2023

A catalogue record for this book is available from the British Library.

ISBN: PB 9781472849137; eBook 9781472849120;
ePDF 9781472849144; XML 9781472849151

23 24 25 26 27   10 9 8 7 6 5 4 3 2 1

Maps by www.bounford.com
Index by Rob Munro
Typeset by PDQ Digital Media Solutions, Bungay, UK
Printed and bound in India by Replika Press Private Ltd.

Osprey Publishing supports the Woodland Trust, the UK's leading woodland conservation charity.

To find out more about our authors and books visit **www.ospreypublishing.com**. Here you will find extracts, author interviews, details of forthcoming events and the option to sign up for our newsletter.

Dedication

This book is dedicated to the members past and present of the White Rose Military Modelling Society.

Author's note

I have visited all the battlefields discussed here in the course of my research and warmly acknowledge the help provided by friendly local guides during the fieldwork trips. I would particularly like to thank Stephen Pow of Saint Petersburg State University (The Russian Science Foundation Project) for so generously sharing his own research into Muhi including translations of Chinese material. One problem with writing about the Mongol invasions is the choice of name to use to identify certain locations where history and politics have combined to provide two, or even three alternatives. The first criterion I have applied here has been to go first for familiarity, hence my use of the German Liegnitz rather than the Polish Legnica. Liegnitz is the German name for the battle, although it is often replaced in German sources by the name Wahlstatt to distinguish it from another battle at Liegnitz that was fought in 1760. The expression 'the battle of Muhi (Mohi or Móhi)' is also more commonly used than 'the battle of the Sajó River' for the Hungarian encounter. My second criterion for less familiar places has been to use the modern-day name of the place so that it may more easily be located on a map. Very few contemporary illustrations exist of the warriors who took part in the campaign on either side. Later representations tend to be based upon written descriptions from the sources noted here, although the arms and armour depicted are often of the artist's own time. Such discrepancies are noted in the captions accompanying illustrations in this book, all of which are from the author's own collection unless otherwise credited.

Artist's note

CONTENTS

INTRODUCTION   **4**

THE OPPOSING SIDES   **10**
Status, recruitment and motivation • Command, control and organization
Weapons and equipment • Battle tactics • Siege warfare

LIEGNITZ   **31**
9 April 1241

MUHI   **46**
1241

ESZTERGOM AND SZÉKESFEHÉRVÁR   **57**
1242

ANALYSIS   **71**

AFTERMATH   **75**

BIBLIOGRAPHY   **78**

INDEX   **80**

Introduction

In the year 1222 a series of ominous and worrying portents began to spread throughout Ruś, the collection of medieval principalities that would one day provide a name for modern-day Russia. A comet appeared in the heavens, while forests and even swamps caught fire in the exceptionally dry summer, producing clouds of smoke so dense that any birds caught in it fell to the ground and died. These events, concluded a later commentator, foretold the invasion by the godless Tartars that would happen a short time later (Dimnik 2003: 292).

The name 'Tartars' was a uniquely European slur that conflated 'Tatar' – a word commonly used from Russia to China and South-East Asia to identify the Mongols – with Tartarus, the Hell of Classical Antiquity. The appellation linking the mysterious and terrible horsemen from the steppes of Central Asia to the underworld was first applied by a Western writer in 1236, although rumours of their conquests in the East had already been circulating for over a decade. Under their inspiring and ruthless leader Chinggis (Genghis) Khan (r. 1206–27) the Mongols had created an empire that had grown rapidly at the expense of its neighbours. The Mongol armies seemed to possess a superhuman capacity for victory, and tales of their cruelty were spread widely and quickly to give the conquerors a psychological advantage over future victims who otherwise knew very little about them. Contemporary European chroniclers only added to this impression of other-worldly invincibility by producing accurate accounts of the Mongols' skills at warfare and then enhancing their narratives with contemptuous and exaggerated descriptions of the Mongols' supposedly monstrous appearance and strange eating habits: matters that were derived not from observation but by associating the Mongols with demonic stereotypes in apocalyptic literature.

The first clash of arms between these frightening beings and the princes of Ruś happened on 31 May 1223 when an expeditionary force under the

Mongol generals Jebe and Sübe'etei was heading back towards Mongolia. Their armies had made the furthest penetration yet towards the West and had ravaged Georgia and the Caucasus. The Mongols encountered the Ruś armies on the banks of the Kalka River, where the Ruś armies were providing assistance to allies from the nomadic confederacy known to the Ruś as the Polovtsy and to other cultures as the Qipchāq or Cumans. The defeat inflicted upon the Ruś/Cuman alliance at the battle of the Kalka River provided a reconnaissance in force for the Mongols that opened up vast areas of Eastern Europe for further conquest.

Apart from a few minor raids after the battle of the Kalka River (which gave a false sense of security when they were successfully resisted), the impression was that the mysterious Mongols had simply disappeared back into Tartary – wherever or whatever that was – leaving the princes of Ruś to their time-honoured tradition of fighting among themselves. The reality was very different. The Mongol withdrawal in 1223 was more akin to the retreat of the first wave of a tsunami that leaves bare the ocean floor and

The head of Duke Henry II, from the copy of his tomb in the Museum of the Battle of Legnica.

then comes crashing back against the land, because in 1237 Ögedei Khan, third son of Chinggis Khan and second emperor of the Mongol empire (r. 1229–41), ordered his forces to return, and the cities of Ruś experienced a Mongol invasion of their own.

The operation against Ruś was the first round of a massive and carefully planned campaign that culminated with the major Mongol offensives into Poland and Hungary in 1241. As the following account will demonstrate, the Mongols' first Eastern European victims were woefully unprepared for the onslaught against them, yet there had been warnings enough if they had cared to listen. In 1223 Rusudan, the queen of Georgia (r. 1223–45), had written to Pope Honorius III to explain why her country had made no contribution towards the Fifth Crusade of 1217–21. The reason was that Georgia had suddenly been ravaged by strange barbarians from the East. As the fresh incursions into Ruś gained momentum urgent reports of the developing situation spread even further west, and included what was now a plea for help from the queen of Georgia rather than just an account of the Mongols' past activity. Even Europe's north-western fringes were touched by anecdotal evidence that something very strange was happening in the East. In his *Chronica Majora* the English Benedictine monk and chronicler Matthew Paris noted that there was a glut in the supply of herring at Yarmouth because traders in the eastern Baltic were afraid to leave their ports owing to some undefined threat. What Paris did not know was that in Eastern Europe that mysterious threat had already became a grim reality (Giles 1889: 131).

The Mongols had displayed a talent for mounted field warfare at the battle of the Kalka River. The new wave of armies fighting in Ruś now had the additional opportunity to demonstrate the techniques of siege warfare which they had absorbed from the Mongol campaigns in China. One by one the Ruś fortresses fell, and after regrouping the Mongol armies pushed on a year later to fight set-piece battles at Liegnitz and Muhi on terrain as steppe-like as anywhere in that part of the world. They then laid siege to the Hungarian royal capital of Esztergom (Gran), and for the first time in history steppe horsemen and European knights fought each other across wooden walls.

Hic ferr capur eiusts duas henia fili sce hedwis i lancea acharris ance castrum legniez

Hic undit in sompnis bea hedwigis animam fily sui duas henrra ducentem ab angelis in paradysum

The earliest-known artistic depiction of the battle of Liegnitz is in the Lubin Codex of 1353. Henry the Pious can be identified by the eagle on his shield. (Anonymous/Wikimedia/Public Domain)

In many ways these encounters proved that the Mongols were even more formidable than anyone in the West had expected. Unlike the Russian experience at Ryazan and Vladimir, however, Esztergom and then Székesfehérvár (Stuhlweißenburg) held off the Mongols in spite of heavy losses, and similar resistance was encountered when the invaders continued their campaign through Croatia to the Adriatic coast. These limited Mongol reverses call into question the traditional view of overwhelming Mongol superiority in the art of war, so in the analysis which follows I shall put to one side this centuries-old assumption about Mongol invincibility. I will instead draw conclusions based on the available evidence, taking into consideration the factors of fortifications and logistics alongside the better-known elements of mobility, skilled archery and terror, and calling into question any simplistic contrast between mobile light Mongols and clumsy heavy European knights.

MAP KEY

Having devastated and secured the main cities of the principalities of Ruś between 1237 and 1238, the Mongols rested before taking Kyiv in 1240 (**1**). After a further pause to regroup at Halych (**2**) separate invasions of Poland and Hungary were launched, although the purpose of the Polish thrust was simply to neutralize any of King Béla IV's supporters who could help him from that direction. In late December 1240 the army destined for Poland headed north and burned Volodymyr-Volynskyi in what is now north-western Ukraine (**3**). The first town to fall to them in Poland was Lublin (**4**), after which the Mongols secured two crossing points of the Wisła River, the first being at Zawichost followed by the important town of Sandomierz (**5**). At some stage in the aforementioned events the Mongols divided their forces and moved west in two main divisions: one towards the Silesian capital of Wrocław (Breslau) and the other against Kraków, the capital of Małopolska (Lesser Poland). The Wrocław division appears to have circled round from the north-east through Wielkopolska (Greater Poland) towards the border with the area then known as Lusatia (Łużyce). The towns of Łeczyca and Sieradz were captured and plundered en route (**6**). The Mongol forces heading for Kraków won a battle at Chmielnik and then joined their comrades in the operation which led to the battle of Liegnitz (**7**). The victorious Mongols traversed Moravia and entered the Kingdom of Hungary through the Hrozenkov Pass around 21 April (**8**). By then the battle of Muhi had taken place.

At about the same time the main body of the Mongol army left Halych in four units for its target of the Kingdom of Hungary, which in the 13th century took in much more than modern-day Hungary and included Transylvania, Croatia and some parts of Austria and Ukraine. The extensive kingdom was protected in the west by the Danube River and at its eastern extremities by the Carpathian Mountains, and one of the earliest precautions the Hungarians took was to build barricades in the mountain passes using felled trees. When the invasion happened these wooden defences would prove to be completely ineffective, however, because the Mongols sent men on ahead with axes to demolish the barricades (HBS: 257–59). Once through the mountain passes the Mongols were able to descend through Transylvania and the Carpathian foothills to the north and spread out across the Great Hungarian Plain, which afforded opportunities for good grazing for their horses and also provided the perfect environment for steppe warfare.

The primary Mongol force under Batu and Sübe'etei employed the shortest route into Hungary by crossing the Verecke Pass (**9**), while the other three armies entered Hungary through Transylvania. The second unit under Qaidan and Büri entered through the Borgó Pass (**10**). The third army under Böchek used the Pass of Oitoz (**11**), and a fourth crossed into Hungary from a southerly direction via the Turnu Roşu Pass (**12**). Advance parties headed for Pest and then led a long feigned retreat that culminated in the battle of Muhi out on the Great Hungarian Plain (**13**). The Mongols then headed back west for the attack on Esztergom (Gran) and other strongpoints, after which their forces merged to pursue the fleeing Hungarian monarch (**14**). The pursuit took them through Croatia to the Adriatic coast near Split (Spalato), after which they withdrew (**15**).

The reason for their apparently abrupt return to Mongolia has traditionally been explained by a need to elect a new khan, a decision that is popularly regarded as having saved Europe. In fact the primary sources suggest that there was no speedy withdrawal; the Mongols took their time, plundering those areas that had remained unscathed when they passed through on their way to Hungary. Their leader Batu never went back to Mongolia. He remained instead in the southern Russian steppes at Sarai on the Volga delta, where he consolidated his position as ruler of the Golden Horde, the power that was to control Russia for more than two centuries. The Golden Horde eventually ruled a region extending from Central Asia to the Dnieper in what is now Ukraine, Russia and Kazakhstan from 1242 until 1480, and it was in the form of the Golden Horde that the Mongols would attack Poland and Hungary again later in the 13th century.

Whatever the real balance of power and skills may have been, Eastern Europe survived in spite of everything, and in the years to come the Hungarian king took stock of his experience and reacted by building more castles and increasing the proportion of heavy knights in his army instead of decreasing it. The reasons why these important strategic decisions were taken will be explained by the following study of the clashes on open plains, across rivers and over city walls that took place between the Mongol horsemen from the steppes and the noble knights of European chivalry.

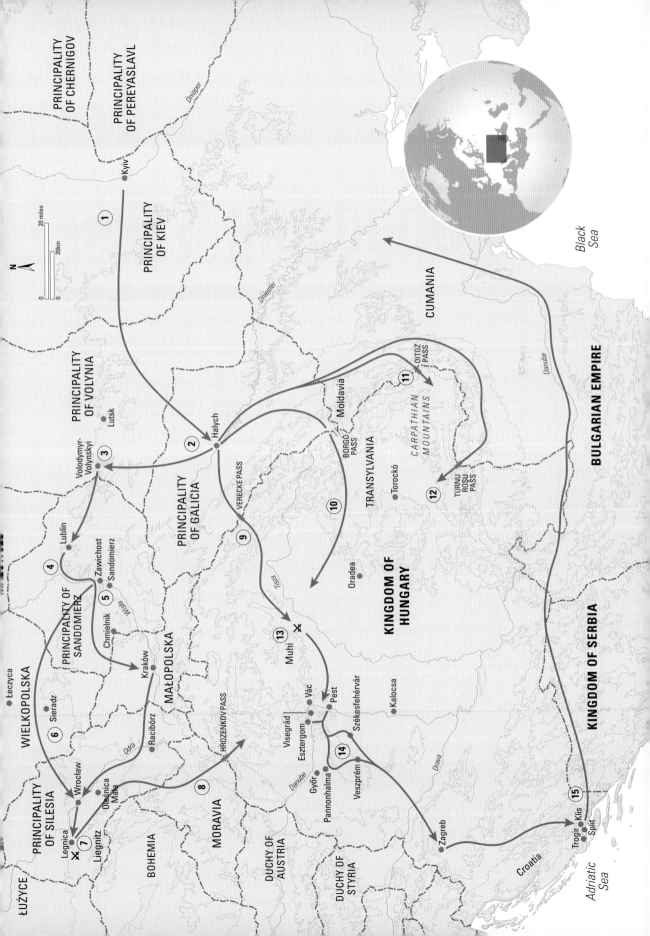

The Opposing Sides

STATUS, RECRUITMENT AND MOTIVATION

The knight

The individuals who confronted the Mongols in Poland and Hungary came from many different origins, and both countries supplied mixtures of nobles, freemen, visiting knights from Western Europe and mercenaries. Their status therefore encompassed a wide social spectrum from the blood royal to feudal levies, with recruitment patterns ranging from an accident of birth to the payment of a mercenary's fee. Overall loyalty and motivation was always to the king in the case of Hungary or to the leader of the individual principality in the case of the knights of Poland and Silesia, although the knights of Hungary would also identify very strongly with their immediate noble leaders, whose views might sometimes be at odds with those of their sovereign. The visiting members of military Orders such as the Templars and Hospitallers followed their own commanders, whose service at Liegnitz and Muhi as allies of the local dignitaries was in line with the Brothers' experience of crusading for a similarly noble cause in the Holy Land.

Most visible on the battlefield within these armies were the heavily armoured and richly apparelled knights. The word 'knight' has a certain romantic air about it that obscures the fact that the man was a specialized fighting machine, and the three encounters described here will illustrate that point very clearly. The exact proportion of knights within the Polish and Hungarian armies is not known. It is likely that the main bodies put into the field by both armies were more lightly armed than the knights and much more numerous, and brave actions by warriors who were neither noble nor knights are definitely confirmed in the chronicles. For example, during the Mongol attack on Sandomierz during the second invasion of Poland in 1259

an ordinary man armed only with a spear and with no body protection other than his cloak killed one Mongol with a single blow of his spear before he was overcome (GVC: 80).

In Hungary there were several ranks of knights. First of all was a socially élite element that included the royal family, the nobility and a handful of fighting bishops who fought as fiercely as anyone else. We will encounter several of these remarkable individuals in the pages which follow. Beneath these aristocratic families were the *servientes regales* (free royal knights) and the lesser landowners known as *iobagiones castri* (castle soldiers), whose feudal rights had been affirmed earlier in the century. These men were all of considerable social status (Ertman 1997: 271–73).

The Mongol warrior

Any social hierarchy that existed within the Mongol armies depended upon the particular individual's relationship to the Khan, but prowess in warfare was very highly valued, and the men who rose to command large units on the battlefield were greatly respected whatever their origins. There was nevertheless a Mongol 'nobility', and the social status of the rest of the army stretched down as far as impressed captives. The highest-ranking Mongol soldiers formed an élite bodyguard for the Great Khan, created originally from the most loyal companions of Chinggis Khan and growing eventually from 150 to 10,000 men. Only nobles and freemen could enter its ranks, and the guardsmen were magnificently equipped and armed. The year 1203 offers the first mention we have of the guard's existence, when 70 men were selected for the *turghaut* (day guard) and 80 men for the *kabtaut* (night guard). Besides these there were 400 *khorchin* (archers) and a personal guard of 1,000 brave men who formed the advance guard in battle. An ordinary soldier in the guard had precedence over a commander in the rest of the army, and the élite guard soon began to play the role of a military academy, so the presence of so many

ABOVE LEFT
An *aquamanile* was a vessel used to pour water over the hands of a priest before he celebrated Mass. Dating from *c.*1250, this specimen depicts a mounted knight. The lance and shield are missing. (metmuseum.org/CC0 1.0)

ABOVE RIGHT
Dating from *c.*1250, this knight chess piece of British manufacture shows the contemporary style of chainmail armour worn underneath a flowing surcoat. (metmuseum.org/CC0 1.0)

This plate shows the arms and personal equipment of the light Mongol horse-archer who, together with the more sturdily armed heavy cavalryman, made up the mounted troops who constituted the Mongol hordes that swept across Central Asia and on into Eastern Europe during the 13th century.

Weapons, dress and equipment

He carries a short Mongol bow (**1**) and a sword (**2**); his bow case (**3**) hangs from his belt. The quiver (**4**) is suspended round his neck and shoulders and hangs at his right side. He wears a coat (**5**) that ties at the right side, heavy trousers (**6**) and lined leather boots (**7**) with thick soles. He has a fur-trimmed felt hat (**8**), an item that frequently appears in contemporary illustrations.

His horse wears characteristic trappings (**9**), and its tail is plaited. The Mongol saddle (**10**) was a very solid affair; made from wood and kept rubbed with sheep fat as a protection against the rain, it was high in the back and at the front, thus providing a secure seat for an archer to discharge his arrows in any direction.

Displayed in the Mongol Invasion Historical Museum, Fukuoka, Japan, this Mongol body armour dates from c.1280. It is made from overlapping leather scales.

potential generals who had trained so close to the Khan made the prospect of future rebellion quite remote.

These fine details were of course unknown to contemporary Western chroniclers, who regarded the Mongols as one vast unregulated horde the numbers of which were immeasurable, an impression that had much to do with their nomadic practice of travelling with a huge body of supporters and family members. The cleric and chronicler Thomas of Split, for example, compared the Mongols to locusts emerging one after another from the ground (HBS: 265). During the second invasion of Hungary in 1285 a different observer would note that the army was so large that it filled a space 9.6km (6 miles) wide and 16km (10 miles) long and took two days to pass any given point. Overwhelming numbers would sometimes be cited as a convenient reason for defeat at the hands of the Mongols, but this was not always the case. At Muhi the Mongols were actually outnumbered by the army they destroyed, although the imagery of vast encompassing hordes persisted everywhere.

COMMAND, CONTROL AND ORGANIZATION

The knight

The Eastern European knights fought under the overall command and leadership of their respective 'royal families'. In the case of Hungary the reigning monarch was the much respected King Béla IV (r. 1235–70), the son of King Andrew II of Hungary (r. 1205–35). Béla had always supported Christian missionary work among the Cumans, some of whose leaders paid sovereignty to him, and he had assumed the title of King of Cumania in 1233. Following Béla and present with him at Muhi was his younger brother Kálmán (Coloman) of Galicia (r. *c.*1215–41), whose name features prominently in the chronicles.

At the time of the Mongol invasion Poland consisted of a number of principalities the rulers of which were rivals as much as allies, but among them were three relatives of King Béla IV of Hungary. They were his son-in-law Bolesław V 'the Chaste' of Sandomierz, his cousin Henry II 'the Pious' of Silesia, and another cousin, Mieszko II 'the Fat', duke of Opole-Racibórz, all of whom would also see action in 1241. Duke Henry II, who was in command at Liegnitz and was killed there, is remembered as something of a saintly figure, hence the title of 'the Pious', which he received posthumously. The knights who served under these royal personages were élite forces through whom royal or noble command and organization was delegated,

Bolesław V 'the Chaste' of Sandomierz is shown on this copy of his tomb in Kraków in the typical armour of a 13th-century knight. When the Mongols attacked his area of Poland Bolesław fled to Hungary, and from thence to Moravia, thus missing the battle of Liegnitz. (Rj1979/Wikimedia/Public Domain)

and it is interesting to note that after the disaster of 1241–42 the Hungarians would place the emphasis on building up their force of heavily armoured knights in the western style, rather than the reverse. From that we may conclude that the classic medieval knights had performed well in spite of everything.

The main bodies of the Polish and Hungarian armies would have been more lightly armed than the knights and were more difficult to organize. Among the Hungarian troops were some light-cavalry archers who were more akin to the Mongols in terms of their origins and *modus operandi*. A 12th-century Moroccan traveller called Abu Hamid al-Gharnati recorded how King Géza II of Hungary (r. 1141–62) had appointed him to recruit groups of horse-archers from the friendly Cumans a century earlier, and a line in the *Galician-Volynian Chronicle* (GVC: 40) notes how the Hungarian archers swooped down on them like hawks, but whether mounted archery was a standard tactic or one confined

With the exception of his crowned helm, the king's overall appearance is typical of the highest-ranking knights of the mid-13th century who would have been seen on the battlefields of Liegnitz and Muhi. The élite knights such as royalty, nobles and their close contingents – along with Western European foreigners, who were quite numerous in the Kingdom of Hungary – would have armour and weapons similar to those used by knights in Western Europe.

Weapons, dress and equipment

The king is armed with a lance (**1**) and broad sword (**2**). His wooden shield (**3**) bears his coat of arms. The all-enclosing helm (**4**) became popular as the century wore on; it was worn over the mail hood (**5**). Body protection was provided by the hauberk, or mail coat (**6**); it reached to knee length and had a hood and mittens. The legs were protected by chausses, mail stockings (**7**). By mid-century there were also defences for the knees and lower legs. Use of the surcoat (**8**) was almost universal; the length varied from knee to ankle length and was split at the front and rear for ease of riding. It was usually a single colour that bore little relation to the coat of arms.

His horse is covered in a trapper or caparison (**9**); these were either in two sections divided at the saddle or occasionally one piece of cloth.

to these eastern mercenaries is open to conjecture. Their presence is also confirmed by a letter from a Hungarian bishop to his French counterpart of about 1239 in which he gives his opinion that the Mongols were better archers than both the Hungarians and the Cumans and had stronger bows (Luard 1882: 75–76).

Not long before the Mongol invasion of 1241 Béla IV had welcomed more Cumans into his army, only to have the process backfire when rumours were spread that the newcomers were in league with the enemy. These false reports may have been based on the fact that some Cumans had been press-ganged into the Mongol armies at an earlier date and were used as forlorn-hope troops in siege warfare operations. In spite of all his pleas, the Cumans' leader Köten was besieged by an angry mob and had his head cut off and thrown out of the palace window. This misguided enmity almost eliminated the sole chance the Hungarians had of fighting alongside loyal warriors who had recent experience of the mounted warfare of the steppes (ESL: 173).

In spite of the prejudice against them some Cumans were allowed to fight for the Hungarians during the campaign, and the remains of two warriors who were probably Cumans have been found in a grave pit associated with the battle of Muhi. A sabretache and scabbard of a knife were attached to the belt of one of the skeletons. There were also the remains of boots, while an octagonal-shaped mace head was found in one grave. Near the other body were found a bridle and eight coins from the years 1235–41. The care given to their internment rules out the victims as being Mongols (Laszlovszky et al. 2016: 33–34).

The Mongol warrior

The Mongol leader of the invasion of Eastern Europe was Batu (r. 1227–55), whose biography appears below. He was well-served by the famous general Sübe'etei, whose military genius probably lies behind many of the moves credited to Batu. The detached Polish campaign was led by Batu's brother Orda and his nephew Baidar, so the princes who led the operation represented all four filial branches of Chinggis Khan's dynasty from his first wife Börte. The mere presence of so many important royal princes and senior generals strongly implies that the Eastern European expedition was no mere raid but a serious attempt at conquest.

Within the Mongol army it was the bond of great personal loyalty rather than kinship that linked these leaders to the captains of *arban* (tens) and the captain of *jaghun* (hundreds), *mingghan* (thousands) and *tumen* (ten thousands), a simple decimal system that facilitated both delegation and communication. In principle the Mongol army was divided into three wings – left, right and centre – plus reserves. Discipline was very strict when these forces went into battle because, whatever may have been the impression given to their victims, the Mongols' military movements were never just lightning-fast sweeps out of the sunset. That terrifying tactic was just the culmination of a longer and slower strategic process, and the final charge against an army or a village settlement would have been merely the death blow.

The experience of a Mongol charge would of course be acutely remembered by any victims who were unaware of the long and slow advance that had preceded it, and the accounts of the movements that preceded the battles of Liegnitz and Muhi reveal complex manoeuvring over a period of many days by armies that advanced separately and then regrouped. All of this was made possible by a superb system of communication between often distant leaders. In order to liaise between separate armies the Mongols set up temporary post stations as they advanced which were manned by several hundred horsemen in a system derived ultimately from the established use of horseback messengers back in Mongolia. The Mongols also made very good use of spies, so they knew the political situation in both Poland and Hungary and kept abreast of any threatening developments or helpful dissension (TR: 98).

The Mongols' nomadic lifestyle required them to graze their horses as they advanced, and the Mongol ponies were adept at extracting the least bit of grass from frozen or snow-covered ground. When on campaign in areas that allowed good grazing the Mongol pattern was to move their animals in the morning, graze them during the afternoon and rest them by night.

This bronze bas-relief commemorates the Mongol invasion of Japan in November 1274, but its depiction of the characteristic heavy coat and boots is in line with the descriptions of the Mongol armies that had ravaged Eastern Europe three decades earlier.

WEAPONS AND EQUIPMENT

The knight

The class distinction noted above for the different ranks of knights was not reflected in their armour and equipment, for which there was great uniformity across Europe, so the types of armour and weapons deployed at Liegnitz or Muhi would not have been distinctly different except in the case of the richer nobility who wished to stand out from the crowd by the newness of design of their apparel. Contingents of Western European foreigners were also quite numerous in Hungary including the military orders, so there were Templars fighting at Liegnitz and Muhi, Hospitallers at Székesfehérvár and Split (Spalato) and at least one Spanish knight at Esztergom. There was therefore a great uniformity to the appearance of the mounted knights, as can be confirmed by investigation of contemporary illustrations and material finds.

John of Plano Carpini, an envoy sent by the Pope Innocent IV to Mongolia after the invasion, is a rich source of information about what these knights needed to fight the Mongols. In the context of this study we must remember that he is writing after the events described below, but it is interesting to see a very similar emphasis being placed by other chroniclers, some of whom were eyewitnesses. The knight, he writes, would need good defensive armour. It should be thick so that arrows did not easily penetrate, together with a helmet and other pieces to protect the body and the horse from their weapons and arrows. He suggests that if some knights were not as well armed as he had described, they should stay behind the others, as the Tartars did, and shoot against them with bows and crossbows (HM: 83).

The basis of the knight's costume was the hauberk (mail coat). It reached to knee length and had a hood and mittens. Part of a knight's hauberk was discovered not far from Muhi. It is thought to have belonged to a retreating Hungarian knight. The legs were protected by chausses (mail stockings), and by mid-century there were also some plate defences for the knees and lower legs. The mail that Polish, German and Hungarian cavalry would have been wearing in this period did not offer great protection against penetrating projectiles like arrows or spears. Pointed projectiles tended to lose relatively little energy piercing the gap between individual links of mail, so it fell to the textile garments worn underneath the armour to defeat missiles by means of their absorption properties. A strapped cuirass worn as an extra protection over the hauberk came into widespread use later in the century, and would probably have been worn by any leader who wished to keep up to date with his choice of armour.

The all-enclosing helm became popular as the century wore on. It was worn over the mail hood and afforded good protection in spite of its obvious drawbacks regarding vision and hearing. The shield was of wood and bore the knight's coat of arms. The use of a surcoat was almost universal; the length varied from knee to ankle length and was split at the front and rear for ease of riding. It was usually a single colour that bore little relation to the coat of arms. The Polish cavalry were required to have a good bow or a strong crossbow (a weapon that the Mongols feared in particular) with

This Western European sword, dating from the 12th or early 13th century, is similar to those used against the Mongols. (metmuseum.org/ CC0 1.0)

This photograph shows a fragment of European chain mail from before 1271 and a spear head of *c*.1270. (metmuseum.org/CC0 1.0)

enough arrows, together with a stout iron axe or a long-handled hatchet. This equipment did not differ significantly from that used by fighting men from the rest of Europe, and the sword that was commonly used was not different from the swords used in the West. The light cavalry who made up the bulk of the Hungarian army had similar levels of protection to their Mongol enemies.

In his descriptions of troops who fought solely on foot, John of Plano Carpini reminds us time and again of the primacy of the crossbow as a weapon for fighting Mongols, stating that whoever wishes to fight the Tartars should have 'a good bow or strong crossbow (which they fear), and enough arrows and a good axe of good iron or a hatchet with a long handle' (HM: 83). The points of the arrows for the bow or crossbow should be tempered in hot water mixed with salt, as the Mongols themselves did, so that they were strong enough to penetrate Mongol armour (HM: 83).

The author of the *Tartar Relation* is even more firmly convinced about the use of crossbows in the field. Crossbowmen, he writes (TR: 100), must be posted in front of the armies in at least three ranks, and must loose their bolts even before they can reach the Mongols' front line, but calmly and at the appropriate time, to prevent their own front ranks from being put to flight or disordered. If the enemy take to flight, the crossbowmen and the archers must pursue them and the army must follow a little way behind, a suggestion that somewhat unwisely makes no consideration of the possibility of a Mongol feigned retreat. If, however, there are no crossbowman to spare, then cavalry with armoured horses must be placed in the vanguard, and these must take cover behind a wall of strong shields (TR: 100).

The Mongol warrior

The classic image of the knights' opponent the Mongol warrior is that of a light mounted archer, a nomad who wore a heavy coat that fastened at the right side, together with heavy trousers and lined leather boots with thick soles. The light cavalryman would normally wear a fur-trimmed felt hat, an item that appears frequently on contemporary western illustrations. Under the outer garments were silk vests, because an arrow hitting silk does not break the fabric but ends up embedding the arrow in the flesh wrapped in silk, allowing the arrow to be removed by gently teasing the silk open. This is opposed to the usual method of removing barbed arrows: cutting them out, or pushing them right through an injured limb and out the other side.

From the archer's belt hung a sword and his bow case containing the short but very powerful Mongol bow. The use of a bow from the saddle was a vital skill, and a quiver full of arrows was suspended round his neck and shoulders and hung at his right-hand side. A round wooden shield provided personal protection against crossbow bolts and also for the occasions when a mounted archer had to engage in hand-to-hand combat. The Mongol archer would then replace his bow within its case and turn to his sword, which had a slight curve like a sabre. Axes and spears were alternative hand weapons, and rounded maces also appear in the written accounts.

The archer would have learned to ride almost as soon as he could walk. His horse wore decorative trappings, and its tail was plaited. The Mongol saddle was a very solid affair; it was made from wood and kept rubbed with sheep fat as a protection against the rain. It was high in the back and at the front, thus providing a secure seat for an archer to discharge his arrows in any direction.

The Mongol heavy cavalryman was also a formidable foe. The armour that he wore over his coat was made in the common Asiatic style of lamellar armour, whereby small scales of iron or leather were pierced with holes and sewn together with leather thongs to make a composite armour plate. A

Dating from *c.*1280, this ornate Mongol helmet has a decorated iron bowl and reinforced leather neck guard. It is displayed in the Mongol Invasion Historical Museum, Fukuoka.

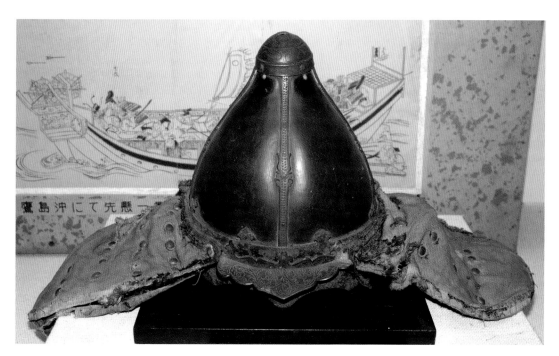

This damaged iron Mongol helmet bowl lacking its neck guard is displayed in the Mongol Invasion Historical Museum, Fukuoka.

leather cuirass of this type weighed about 8kg (17.6lb). Alternatively, a heavy coat could be reinforced using metal plates, while the same heavy leather boots noted above were worn on the feet. The helmet, which was made from a number of larger iron pieces, was roughly in the shape of a rounded cone and had the added protective feature of a neck guard of iron plates. Some of the Mongol heavy cavalry rode horses that also enjoyed the protection of lamellar armour.

Mongol heavy armour is mentioned in a reference of 1252 to the army of Prince Danilo of Galicia who had been forced to accept overlordship from the Mongols' Golden Horde. The Germans who saw Danilo's army marvelled at their Tartar-style armour: all the horses had mail over their heads while their flanks were covered with leather, and the riders also wore armour (GVC: 61). Mongol heavy cavalrymen used swords and maces and also carried spears, and their use of the latter weapons in hand-to-hand fighting is attested for the siege of Sandomierz in 1259–60. Having climbed over the shattered walls the Mongols moved through the city streets, slashing at people with their swords and running them through with their spears (GVC: 79–80).

BATTLE TACTICS

The knight

During the 13th century knightly tactics on the battlefield were by no means elaborate, and the cherished ideal celebrated in chivalric romance was to achieve a dramatic victory by the shock delivered using a heavy cavalry charge. In preparation for their assault the knights stayed in closed formation along with their squires with infantry on their flanks and began charging after an initial discharge of arrows and bolts by archers and crossbowmen. The advance would begin at a walk, with the speed of the charge increasing through a canter to a final gallop so that the horses were not exhausted before contact was made. The line of knights then drew near to their enemies, the aim being to deliver a powerful blow from a mass of knights riding almost knee to knee with their lances lowered, at which any enemy units on foot should be expected to break, leaving individuals prey to the tips of the lances. That was the ideal outcome, but it was a tactic that demanded the strictest group discipline and required of the individual knight a consummate skill at couching his lance while correctly using his shield as protection against the expected hail of Mongol arrows. An ill-conducted charge would leave the charging knights vulnerable to a counter-attack in flank and a disastrous reversal. That would be a moment of great danger, and the leader of the detachment, who always fought at the head of his men, could lose control over his subordinate knights. There might then be the possibility of disorder and even panic, and any advantage gained from the charge would be lost. This was a factor the Mongols loved to exploit by using their tactic of a feigned retreat, as discussed below. Other counter tactics were developed around trying to either make it impossible for the knights to hit them with a charge, or get the knights to waste their energies before the Mongols launched a counter-attack.

By this time in the battle the knight's helmet would have grown hot, restricting his vision and muffling the sounds of the conflicts taking place all

Weighing 43g, this Austrian prick spur is made from iron alloy and dates from the mid-12th to the mid-13th centuries. Spurs were closely associated with cavalry warfare and become one of the symbols of chivalry throughout Christian Europe. (metmuseum.org/CCO 1.0)

around him, but if he became disorientated a knight would look for his lord's banner as a rallying point. The lances would often shatter on impact when individual contact was made, leaving the knights to draw their swords or wield their maces. Sword-fighting by knights was always conceived of in terms of a combination of sword and shield. Offensive blows would be directed at weak points in an opponent's armour such as an unguarded face, while defensive tactics against sword strokes depended upon using the shield and having one's own sword ready for a counterstroke. Chain mail could be broken by a fiercely delivered sword blow, or even driven into the knight's flesh, which could cause some very nasty wounds.

The goad of this 12th-century prick spur from Central Europe is shaped like a flower and features an incised decorative pattern more elaborate on its right branch, indicating that it is for the owner's right heel. (metmuseum.org/CC0 1.0)

The Mongol warrior

Mongol tactics were very different from those of the knights and drew upon the warriors' mobility and flexibility. The process of enveloping and surrounding an army was a favourite Mongol ploy, and it would be over a century before a European army managed to overcome a Mongol attempt at envelopment. That was at the battle of Kulikovo in 1380 where forests and rivers provided secure limits for the rear and flanks of the Russian army, thus preventing the Mongols of the Golden Horde from encircling them. If an enemy stood on the defensive in a field position and refused to budge the Mongols would pull back the main body of their troops and leave smaller detachments to harass the enemy lines. In time a lack of food and water would compel the enemy to move, whereupon the Mongol scouts would communicate this intelligence back to the main body so that the Mongols could catch the enemy in the open.

The other great Mongol battlefield tactic was the use of a feigned retreat, enticing a distant enemy to follow them to ground of the Mongols' own choosing. John of Plano Carpini wrote that they did this to make the enemy follow them as far as the places where they had prepared ambushes (HM: 68 & 84). At the battlefield level the feigned retreat was set in motion by throwing an advance guard forward. When hostile contact was made the feigned retreat began, pulling the enemy further and further into the embrace of the wings that were already being extended forward to catch them, and at the right moment the retreating force would turn about and join in the attack.

The Italian prelate Master Roger, archbishop of Split from 1249 until his death in 1266, records another clever ruse that the Mongols supposedly put into operation just before the battle of Muhi. Noting that the Mongols always took along more horses as spare mounts, they created what Master Roger describes (ESL: 178) as '*larvas et monstra quamplurima*' ('many ghostly monstrous figures'), which they sat on the riderless horses. Servants led this ghostly army behind the main body that was outnumbered by the Hungarians. The Mongols then feigned retreat, at which point the Hungarians caught sight of what was apparently a huge reserve force. Fearing a trap, they prudently withdrew.

According to the *Tartar Relation*, when the Mongols drew near to their enemies they sent their swiftest skirmishers on ahead to spread terror, to kill individuals and to hinder their enemy's mobilization. If success was gained in such minor skirmishes when enemies were encountered the Mongols would press further on, leaving reserves stationed in their rear. If, however, neither enemies nor obstacles were encountered they simply continued to advance along with all their baggage train without any attempt at concealment. If they encountered resistance and also perceived that the enemy were too numerous to defeat, the Mongols immediately withdrew to the main body and drew up their forces with the mass of the main body grouped around their standard in the middle. They placed one force on each wing at a small distance away but projecting far forward from the main body. Finally, a small detachment began guarding the baggage train and the Mongol families located to the rear. The Mongols were now prepared for battle.

Whatever preliminary tactics of envelopment or feigned retreat may have been put into operation, at some stage the two armies would close. When they were on the point of confrontation a number of Mongol archers, each

This curious wooden statue of a Mongol warrior stands within the grounds of the Museum of the Battle of Legnica, which was formerly a church said to have been founded by Duke Henry II's mother. The figure wears the shoulder guards of a Mongol heavy cavalryman.

equipped with several quivers full of arrows, began to shoot as a means of intimidation before their enemies had a chance to respond, even commencing their volleys while they were still out of range. As soon as they were close enough for the arrows to hit their mark the archers began firing dense volleys, a characteristic tactic noted by several commentators, all of whom use expressions translatable as 'a rain of arrows' because of the density of the fire.

The stage was now set for hand-to-hand combat. The Mongol heavy cavalry would probably dominate such situations, including any counter-attack. This phase of a Mongol battle has often been dismissed in the past as being less important than the effects of archery, but no Mongol

battle was ever won by archery alone. In these mêlée actions we must discard the traditional image of the Mongol light archers and see them instead joining the well-protected heavy horsemen to attack with spears, swords and maces and defending themselves with their shields. There are few descriptions of how the spear was actually used, but various miniature paintings suggest that it could either be couched like a lance or wielded as a stabbing weapon, although there are a few references to javelins, which suggests that the spears would also be thrown. Such a mêlée was never wholly disorganized. It was always the plan that an unprepared enemy should be almost completely surrounded leaving only one obvious escape route to be exploited later. The Mongols would then attack fiercely so that anyone who was not killed in position would be cut down at leisure when he tried to flee. This tactic was used at Muhi where the only obvious escape route led towards a marshy area.

The fortified stone church of St Andrew in Kraków sheltered the only survivors when the Mongols attacked the city on 22 March 1241. It was a minor lesson in the importance of stone defences.

SIEGE WARFARE

The knight

During the Mongol campaigns much time was spent in the attack and defence of fortified places. The siege experience in Central Asia had been a series of Mongol triumphs, but the author of the *Tartar Relation* still suggests optimistically that cities and fortified places should be able to hold out against the Mongols in spite of arrows loosed and missiles hurled from siege engines. If supplies of food, drink or firewood gave out, claims the chronicler, then the courage and daring of the defenders alone would triumph. To back this up he gives the example of some unidentified people he calls the 'Old Saxons' who were besieged by the Mongols. While the men defended the city walls the women extinguished fires in the burning town. Some brave souls sallied out repeatedly, and the defenders even halted a Mongol attempt at infiltration via an underground passage. The *Tartar Relation* also stresses the use of crossbowmen in siege situations (TR: 98–100). John of Plano Carpini too has much to say in a similar vein about siege work: defenders should fight back with crossbows and slings and catapults so that the Tartars do not approach the city (HM: 86).

The Mongol warrior

By the time of the invasion of Hungary Mongol siege warfare had become very sophisticated, and the development of Mongol siege craft provides an outstanding example of how the Mongols were willing and able to learn from

In this later reproduction of a miniature painting the walls of Legnica are being defended against the Mongols, who are parading the severed head of Duke Henry II. The defenders are shown using the key weapon that every commentator recommends against the Mongols: the crossbow.

the people they had conquered. Their first teachers were Chinese artisans, and successive Khans always spared usefully talented individuals from being massacred when a city fell. The Mongols' reputation for capturing fortified places had grown rapidly almost from their first campaign against the Xi Xia (Tanguts) of north-western China when they built a dyke to flood out their enemies. As early as 1224 we read of the Mongols digging a mine under the Xi Xia fortress of Shazhou and using catapults. At Kuju in Korea in 1231 the Mongols loaded carts with grass and wood and overturned them beside the gates so that fires could be started, so even though sedentary city dwellers were confronted by what appeared to be a mounted and mobile nomad army it was never an option for cities simply to close their gates and hope the Mongols would go away.

Bombardment was used if cities did not surrender to immediate assault. Catapult artillery was employed in the form of traction trebuchets, which were much more mobile than the heavy counterweight variety, and needed to be resisted by equally good defences. Some preventative measures were quite simple, albeit laborious. For example, the inhabitants of one city in Central Asia that was targeted for attack not only laid waste the countryside for 10km (6 miles) around but also carefully removed every stone they could find so that they could not be used as catapult ammunition. There was a similar shortage of stones during another campaign. We are not told if this was deliberate, but the Mongol artillerymen used instead balls of mulberry wood, hardened by soaking them in water.

Ryazan was but one place among many in Ruś that the Mongols surrounded by constructing a stout palisade to confine the inhabitants within (CN: 82). Otherwise battering rams and countless scaling ladders were put in place. In Hungary seven siege engines battered Oradea until the newly built city wall collapsed entirely (ESL: 201). Thirty siege engines were deployed to capture Esztergom, where prisoners were forced to

This vivid oil painting in Sandomierz cathedral shows the massacre of the Dominicans by the Mongols in 1259. An angel descends from above the slaughter to present the crown of martyrdom to the victims.

build a protective wall from bundles of wood, behind which the catapults bombarded the city (ESL: 217).

Yet the Mongol catapults were not infallible, as a fascinating anecdote in the Galician-Volynian Chronicle shows. During the 1240 campaign in Ukraine the Mongols attacked the town of Łuck (Lutsk), to which many people had fled for refuge even though it was not fortified. The Styr River was high and impossible to cross, so the townspeople began to destroy the only bridge. The Mongols set up some catapults in an attempt to drive the defenders away from the riverbank. The catapults were traction trebuchets and at that point, says the chronicler, a divine miracle occurred. The author claims that the wind was so strong that when the catapults hurled their missiles at the inhabitants by the bridge, each stone was blown back against the Tartars who had flung it. In the end the catapults broke down, which suggests that the reality of the situation was that, rather than being blown by the wind (which is highly unlikely), the missiles were being delivered with insufficient force to complete their arcs of travel and instead fell back on to the traction trebuchets that had thrown them. This might also suggest that the traction trebuchets were being operated by untrained captives (GVC: 74–75).

At some stage an armed assault would be made over the shattered defensive walls, and a common Mongol practice was to send captives on ahead of the actual Mongol army. The tasks these unfortunates were given included filling up moats, erecting siege engines under fire and even taking part in storming parties. Only a few Mongol leaders were needed to supervise these forlorn-hope troops, who unintentionally provided human shields for the Mongols because it was expected that the defenders would be reluctant to fire upon their own people, thus making the Mongol advance that much easier.

Liegnitz

9 April 1241

BACKGROUND TO BATTLE

The Mongols' Eastern European campaign was launched by the invasion of Ruś in 1237. The operation is well recorded, and the chroniclers' doom-laden introductions to the events are all much the same. For example, the *Chronicle of Novgorod* notes (CN: 81) that in the same year foreigners called Tartars came into the land of Ryazan in countless numbers like a swarm of locusts. The city of Ryazan fell on 21 December 1237, followed by the then minor city of Moscow and afterwards Vladimir and Suzdal. By the end of February 1238, 14 Ruś strongpoints had been taken, concluding with Torzhok on 5 March, where the gates managed to withstand the Mongol battering rams for two weeks (CN: 83). The Mongols then paused to rest, probably because they were waiting for reinforcements, and the remainder of that year saw only minor troop movements on their part while King Béla IV of Hungary provided asylum to tens of thousands of Cumans who had fled from the Tartar advance.

A statue of the fully armoured Duke Henry II on the outside wall of Wrocław cathedral.

The next event of major military significance was Batu's capture of Kyiv. This was the culmination of the operations in Ukraine where one could not hear anything as a result of the great noise caused by the screeching carts, the countless grunting camels and the neighing teams of horses (GVC: 44). The city succumbed to sustained catapult bombardment on 6 December 1240 after many instances of heroism by the defenders. Batu's triumph was followed by the reduction of certain smaller towns in preparation for the invasion of Hungary.

The campaign that then began was a classic example of a long-range and well-planned effort on a massive scale. The Kingdom of Hungary was the Mongols' primary objective – the help King Béla IV had given to the Cumans was regarded by the Mongol leaders as a serious provocation – and the purpose of the separate Polish thrust that culminated at Liegnitz on 9 April 1241 was to neutralize support. Yet so extensive were the Mongols' military resources that to all intents and purposes the Polish and the Hungarian campaigns can be regarded as separate operations.

By using the Polish priest and chronicler Jan Długosz as our main guide and supplementing his narrative with fragments from other sources the overall course of the Mongol advance into Poland can be reconstructed with some confidence. In late December 1240 the invading army burned Volodymyr-Volynskyi in what is now north-west Ukraine. After destroying Lublin the Mongols secured the Wisła (Vistula) River at Zawichost and Sandomierz, the latter of which capitulated on 13 February 1241 after an initial repulse of the Mongol assault by its brave citizens. The Mongol forces then moved west towards the Silesian capital of Wrocław (Breslau) and Kraków, the capital of Małopolska (Lesser Poland). The Wrocław operation was under the command of Batu's brothers Orda and Qaidan, and they appear to have circled round roughly in the direction of modern-day Warsaw, taking Łeczyca and Sieradz.

The Mongol forces heading for Kraków were under the command of Baidar, but the noble knights of Małopolska attempted to block his advance by making a stand at the village of Chmielnik near Szydłow. Długosz's account of the battle of Chmielnik makes it sound like a dress rehearsal for the great battle of Liegnitz that was to happen soon afterwards. The fighting began as the sun rose on 18 March 1241. The Poles drew up in a single line with no reserves, and after many brave exchanges it appeared that they had driven the Mongols back. Yet their elation would be short-lived, because fresh troops from the Mongol reserves took up the attack, a sequence of events which probably indicates that the Mongols had set in motion their classic ruse of a feigned retreat. The Poles were tired and many were wounded. Some fled the battlefield to reach the cover of woods and managed to escape because of their familiarity with the terrain, but most

BELOW LEFT
The city of Sandomierz, with its valuable river crossing, capitulated on 13 February 1241 after an initial repulse of the Mongol assault by its brave citizens.

BELOW RIGHT
As the Mongols approached Kraków the knights of Małopolska (Lesser Poland) attempted to block their advance by making a stand at the village of Chmielnik near Szydłow. Many were killed during the ensuing battle.

found a glorious death in combat and the noblest of their knights perished to a man. Kraków was now wide open to attack and fell on 22 March, with only a few defenders escaping death because they had locked themselves inside the fortified stone church of St Andrew. The rest of the population had already fled (AJD: 178).

This Mongol army then headed north from Kraków to join their comrades who were already bearing down upon Wrocław, destroying on their way the commandery of the Knights Templar at Oleśnica Mała, which was located 36km (22 miles) to the south-east of Wrocław (Burzyński 2012: 59). The Templars who escaped would take part in the battle of Liegnitz. This particular Mongol advance seems to have been carried out by a number of separate groups, one unit of which had a minor reversal on the way when they suffered a defeat at the hands of Duke Mieszko II 'The Fat' as they crossed the Odra (Oder) River near Racibórz. The town had been burnt by its inhabitants when they left and all the bridges were destroyed, so the crossing was made using improvised rafts or by swimming, an art at which the Mongols were expert, according to Długosz. As well as inflicting perhaps 400 casualties on the Mongols the victory bought time for Duke Henry II 'The Pious' to rally his troops in Silesia, and when more Mongols appeared Mieszko's army headed north to join his cousin's force. On 2 April the two Mongol armies combined to attack Wrocław. The city was set on fire, either by the Mongols or by its own terrified citizens who had abandoned their homes and taken refuge on an island in the Odra (AJD: 178). The tiny church of St Giles is the only survivor to this day of the Mongol attack on the city.

ABOVE LEFT
The cathedral of Wrocław (Breslau), which also fell to the Mongol advance through Poland. Some survivors took refuge on an island in the Odra (Oder) River, showing the advantage of having a water barrier against the Mongols.

ABOVE RIGHT
The tiny church of St Giles is the only ecclesiastical building in Wrocław to have survived the Mongol attack.

MAP KEY

1 Duke Henry II's army advances from Legnica castle.

2 Henry selects his ground and sets up his battle line.

3 The Mongol army takes up positions around the hill of Grodzisko, with some units being kept back on lower ground to the rear.

4 The Mongol left wing crosses the Księginice Stream and engages the Polish right.

5 The Poles appear to be winning but a feigned retreat is set up and Henry's army advances in pursuit.

6 Duke Mieszko II leaves the battlefield.

7 The armies engage under the cover of a smokescreen set up by the Mongols.

8 More Mongols come from the rear to reinforce the attack and carry out an envelopment.

9 The Polish army is pursued in the direction of Legnickie Pole.

10 Henry is surrounded and killed.

Battlefield environment

The battle of Liegnitz was fought on open ground near Legnica, where fields and minor roads still allow one to appreciate terrain that may not have been very different in 1241. The low rounded hills are easily identifiable and the only major modern additions are a number of wind turbines. The Wierzbak River flows in a westward then northwards direction round the town of Legnickie Pole to the south to provide an outer limit for the battlefield area. Duke Henry II's army advanced from Legnica castle towards the south-east along the course of a minor road that heads to Księginice via Bartoszów and crosses the Wierzbak. It is assumed that because the Mongols were advancing from the north-east Henry's army took up a good position to the south of this road, setting up a battlefront looking north-east that made use of the higher ground and was anchored on Księginice at the extremity of its right flank. In front of Henry was lower ground crossed by a brook called the Księginice Stream which flowed ultimately into Lake Koskowickie and provided a minor barrier between his army and the approaching Mongols. The eastern end of this area is marshy to this day, but there are no records of swampy ground hindering either side's advance in 1241.

The Mongol army was approaching from Wrocław, and on seeing Henry's army the Mongols are believed to have turned to face south-west in the direction of Legnickie Pole from high ground around the 152m (499ft) hill of Grodzisko along the line of the modern Legnica–Wrocław road. The main fighting took place in the fields between the stream and the road below. The village of Legnickie Pole, where Henry's decapitated body would be found when his defeated army retreated, lies to the rear of the Polish positions and the towers of its abbey can be seen over the horizon from the battlefield, from which Legnickie Pole is now separated by the course of the modern A4 highway.

The battlefield of Liegnitz, looking eastwards to the hill of Grodzisko, the probable centre of the Mongol lines.

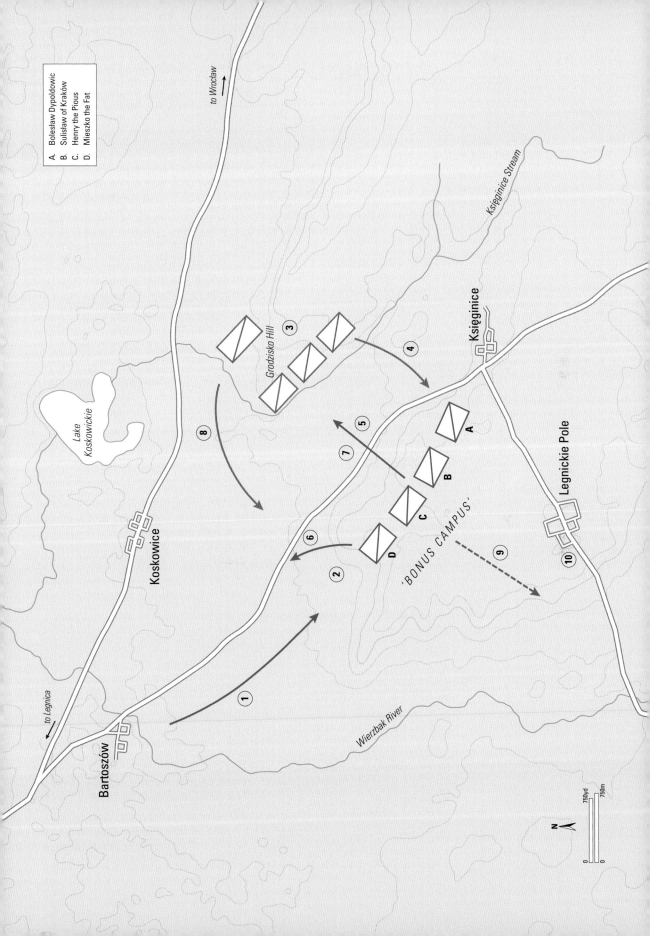

A. Bolesław Dypoldowic
B. Sulisław of Kraków
C. Henry the Pious
D. Mieszko the Fat

to Wrocław

Księginice Stream

Grodzisko Hill

Księginice

Lake
Koskowickie

A

B

7

5

4

3

8

C

'BONUS CAMPUS'

Legnickie Pole

D

6

2

9

10

Koskowice

1

to Legnica

Bartoszów

Wierzbak River

N

750yd

750m

INTO COMBAT

On 9 April 1241 Duke Henry II gave battle at Liegnitz without waiting for reinforcements from his father-in-law King Wenceslaus (Václav) I of Bohemia (r. 1230–53), whose involvement might have saved the day. As it was Henry commanded at least 2,000 men with an upward limit of 4,000 against between 6,000 and 10,000 Mongols. Nevertheless, Henry rode out from Legnica castle brimming with confidence, only to suffer an immediate bad omen when a stone fell from the roof of the church of the Blessed Virgin and narrowly missed his head.

It was a divine warning at the very least, notes Długosz, who is very unhelpful when it comes to envisaging the army's layout, because his 'ranks' are no more than the units that followed the line of march from Legnica. Długosz writes (AJD: 178) that crusaders and volunteers who spoke several languages made up the first rank along with some gold miners from Złotoryja (Goldberg) who were under the overall command of Bolesław Dypoldowic 'the Lisper'. There is a plaque on the wall of the battlefield museum commemorating these men. In the second rank were knights from Wielkopolska (Greater Poland), while in the third rank were the knights drawn from Opole-Racibórz. Długosz's next rank appears to have consisted of high-ranking nobility, because they are described as the barons of Wrocław and other places in Silesia together with the pick of other knights under the command of Henry himself, along with some mercenaries who may have been the much-valued crossbowmen.

Długosz also adds a contingent consisting of what he calls Prussian knights, a contingent traditionally identified as the Teutonic Order, although the presence of any Teutonic Knights at Liegnitz has now been disproved. Strangely, Długosz does not mention by name the Templars whose presence has been confirmed by a letter sent to King Louis IX of France (r. 1226–70) from their Grand Master Ponces d'Aubon. He reports that nine senior brother knights took part in the battle, of whom six were killed and three survived. They were accompanied by about 30 others of lower rank and a local contingent drawn from the Templars' Polish estates. Military service was compulsory for village headmen, who were required to bring along their *poczet* (a unit of armed warriors). Assuming that about 12 village headmen joined in, it has been estimated that the Templar contingent at Liegnitz must have consisted in total of between 68 and 88 men. The Grand Master's letter, however, refers to the Order suffering 500 casualties, a figure that must include all those killed on Templar lands during the entire campaign, including the destruction of their headquarters at Oleśnica Mała (Burzyński 2012: 60).

Duke Henry II drew up his army near Legnickie Pole at a spot called, in the original Latin, 'Bonus Campus' (The Good Field). According to the battlefield dispositions accepted by the Museum of the Battle of Legnica at Legnickie Pole, the left wing was held by the knights of Opole-Racibórz who fought under Duke Mieszko II. On the far-right flank stood the contingent of Bolesław 'the Lisper' who had led the march from Legnica. Beside them towards the centre were knights under a Moravian *émigré* in Henry's court called Sulisław of Kraków,

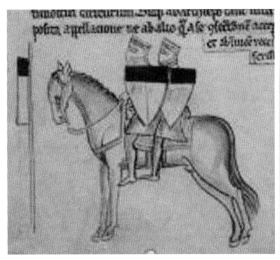

whose brother Włodzimerz had been killed at the battle of Chmielnik. Next along stood Henry with the nobles of Silesia and Wrocław, among whom a persistent local tradition identifies a group of Silesian knightly families who became known as the 'Cousins of Wahlstatt'. One knight with the surname of Rothkirch acted as Henry's standard bearer and was killed during the battle. When Rothkirch's son was born fatherless the following year members of the Nostitz, Prittwitz, Zedlitz, Seydlitz and Strachwitz families, each of which are said to have lost at least one family member in the encounter, swore to support him. It is more than likely that these knights would have been seen on the battlefield in very close proximity to Henry.

The Mongol army which, notes Długosz, was more numerous and more experienced in battle than the hosts who faced them, started the battle. The Mongols first sent some troops across the Księginice Stream against Bolesław 'the Lisper', who was killed when an arrow hit him under the ear. Henry responded with a charge that broke through the first rank of the Mongols, but we may perhaps understand this scenario as the light Mongol horsemen deliberately allowing the heavy knights to pass through them as part of the tactic of envelopment, because we then read that the Poles were surrounded by Mongol archers who harassed them and prevented other knightly contingents from coming to their aid. They fell beneath a hail of arrows as if a hailstorm had smashed delicate heads of corn (AJD: 179).

Somehow the Poles rallied, and it would appear that this was because their crossbowmen had moved into action and were bringing down Mongol horsemen as both sides engaged along the line. This was most encouraging, but just then great confusion began, because someone emerged from the Mongol ranks. The individual shouted 'Run, run!' to the Poles and encouraged the Mongols' efforts. His cries were heard by Duke Mieszko II, on the left flank of Duke Henry II's army, who thought that the man was a friend giving a warning, so he withdrew his men from the field and headed back to Legnica. Henry, however, realized that the incident was instead a deliberate trick on the part of the Mongols and rallied his unit. They were the élite knights

ABOVE LEFT
Two Templars share one horse in this illustration from Matthew Paris's *Chronica Majora*. Note the helmets with face plates, the uniform, simple shield designs and the absence of horse trappings. (Fine Art Images/Heritage Images/Getty Images)

ABOVE RIGHT
The battlefield of Liegnitz, looking across the area of lower ground from the likely position of the right wing of the Polish army.

First contact at Liegnitz, 9 April 1241

Mongol view: This scene depicts the moment at the battle of Liegnitz when the two armies of mounted warriors meet at close range for the first time. The Mongols are now within deadly bowshot range of the Silesian knights. The Mongol smokescreen has confused their enemies while reducing the visibility, but the knights' armour and brightly coloured shields present a sufficient target for the hails of arrows that the Mongol light cavalrymen are now discharging. Their determined-looking mounted archers are of a largely uniform appearance as they pull arrows rapidly from their quivers, but one of the group wears heavy armour. He is the bearer of the *tug* standard.

Knights' view: Their lances ready for a charge, Duke Henry II and his fellow knights from Silesia are met by a furious hail of Mongol arrows. Their view of the approaching Mongols is partly obscured by a dense smokescreen produced by burning reeds, above which the Mongol *tuk* standard can be seen. In addition to the duke, the individual knights depicted here are those traditionally known as the 'Cousins of Wahlstatt'. Prominent among them is a knight from the Rothkirch family, who was Henry's standard bearer. Identified by his blazonry of three lions' heads, he carries the banner into battle. His comrades are shown from left to right as Strachwitz, Nostitz, Seydlitz, Prittwitz and Zedlitz.

and the best of his troops, and at one point they seemed to be winning, but just as they appeared to have overcome the invaders a fourth Mongol unit arrived and for a while honours were even among the deadly hand-to-hand fighting (AJD: 179–80). This sequence of events is also suggested in the *Tartar Relation*, because the author was told that at this stage in the battle the Mongols were on the point of flight but that the columns of the Christians then unexpectedly turned and fled (TR: 80).

The flight mentioned in the *Tartar Relation* is a brief reference to what would prove to be the pivotal moment of the battle of Liegnitz. The episode is commemorated by a fresco on the ceiling of the Benedictine abbey at Legnickie Pole, which depicts the battle standard of the Mongols as a curious device with an animal's head out of which smoke is pouring. This imagery derives from the chronicle of Długosz, who mentions that among the Tartar standards was a huge one with a giant 'X' painted on it. It was topped by an ugly black head with a chin covered in hair. Długosz claims that the 'great head' was shaken violently, at which a foul-smelling cloud burst forth and enveloped the Polish knights, making them faint and rendering them incapable of fighting.

Here Długosz is probably combining two developments in the battle. The first is the deployment of the *tug* (Mongol standard) as a rallying point. The precise design of the standard at Liegnitz is unknown except for Długosz's description but, judging by later examples, it most probably featured plumes of black yak hair. The other development was the creation of a medieval version of a smokescreen, which was probably produced by burning bundles of reeds to cover the Mongol advance across the fields. The smoke would have made the knights choke and also irritated their eyes (AJD: 180).

Długosz reckons that the smoke emerging from the standard was the result of witchcraft, an art at which the Mongols excelled. Magic or not, it certainly caused problems for the knights, so the Mongols took advantage of their discomfort and attacked them all the more fiercely, scattering the ranks that up until then had held firm and beginning a very great slaughter. Henry is commended by Długosz for his bravery in this situation because he did not desert his men. Instead he and a handful of knights were surrounded but tried to force their way through the Mongol ranks. The move almost succeeded, but the carnage was extensive and soon Henry had only four knights left alive to accompany him. At that point his own horse dropped dead. A brave follower brought him a fresh

The battlefield of Liegnitz, looking from the general area of the Mongol lines towards the ridge along which Duke Henry II arranged his army.

horse and Henry remounted in an attempt to try to break out again, but once again he was closely surrounded. As Henry lifted his arm to bring his sword down against an enemy a Mongol heavy cavalryman thrust his spear into the duke's armpit, at which he slid from his horse seriously wounded. Henry was recognized by his heraldry, so other Mongols pounced on his body and dragged him two bowshots clear of the mêlée. There they cut off his head, tore off all his distinguishing marks from his clothing, and left his corpse naked and exposed. Many other nobleman, writes Długosz, found a similar martyrdom.

The *Tartar Relation* account of Henry's death is slightly different. In this version Henry was captured, but before he was executed the Mongols stripped him completely naked and made him kneel in front of the body of their general who had been killed at Sandomierz. Presumably the said general's corpse was being conveyed to Mongolia for burial. After the battle the Mongols took Henry's head with them through Moravia into Hungary to Batu and threw it among the other heads of the slain as if it had been the head of a sheep (TR: 80–82).

Długosz also celebrates Jan Iwanowic, the knight who brought Henry the replacement horse that nearly saved him. Iwanowic subsequently joined

The battle of Liegnitz from the *Baumgarten Legend* by an unknown artist of 1504. The Mongols are shown in contemporary armour but with their characteristic Mongol caps for identification. Duke Henry II is killed in the foreground.

Duke Henry II's mother finds his body. This picture is also from the *Baumgarten Legend*, and with this scene the story of the discovery of Henry's body is incorporated into the canon for the first time. The *Baumgarten Legend* had the underlying motive of rousing sentiments against the Turks, who were Christendom's enemies when it was painted.

forces with five other survivors including a knight called Lucman who had two servants with him and had suffered 12 wounds. When their Mongol pursuers paused for breath in a village a short distance from the battlefield, the six turned and attacked them, killing two of their number and taking one Mongol prisoner. After this, Iwanowic entered a Dominican monastery and lived piously as a monk for the rest of his life, grateful that God had saved him from so many dangers (AJD: 180).

When the battle was over the Mongols collected some booty and attempted to ascertain the exact number of Polish dead by cutting off one ear from each corpse they found. They filled nine huge sacks to the brim with the mementoes. With Duke Henry II's head impaled on a long lance, they approached the castle at Legnica (the town has already been burned for fear of the Mongols) and displayed it for all those inside to see, calling upon them through an interpreter to open the gates. Henry's headless body had been left on the battlefield where it was found later by his grieving mother who had scoured the area looking for him. She managed to identify his ill-treated corpse only by the six toes on his left foot, a distinguishing feature that was confirmed when his tomb was opened in 1832.

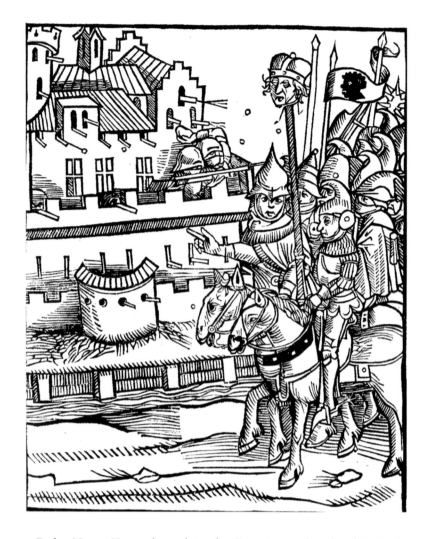

A woodcut of 1504 from the *Baumgarten Legend* showing the Mongols displaying Duke Henry II's head outside the castle of Legnica, which is shown being defended with firearms!

Duke Henry II was buried in the Franciscan church of St Hedwig (nowadays St Vincent's) in Wrocław where his fine effigy (which is now in the National Museum in Wrocław) was given a defeated Mongol under his feet. According to legend, Henry's mother also arranged for a church to be erected on the spot where his body was found; it is now in the Museum of the Battle of Legnica. It is more likely to be a later foundation, but records show that masses were offered there for the victims of Liegnitz until the Reformation. Duke Henry II would be revered as a Christian hero for centuries to come, and a modern-day stained-glass window in Wrocław cathedral depicts him in the company of the three saints who are the patrons of Wrocław and Silesia.

Following their great victory the Mongol army withdrew from Poland, their aim having been to make sure that no reinforcements from the region distracted the ongoing operations in Hungary. That objective had been completely fulfilled by the triumph at Liegnitz, so the Mongol army had no reason to stay and headed south to join their comrades in Hungary. There were some skirmishes on the Austrian border along the way, as is confirmed by a letter of 13 July 1241 in which Duke Frederick II of Austria claims a victory over the Mongols on his borders as the invaders made their way towards Hungary. Some 300 Mongols were killed, and the report was followed by another letter two weeks stating that 700 Mongols had been killed in a separate encounter.

At the time of the battle of Liegnitz King Wenceslaus I of Bohemia had only been about two days' march away with his knights, but when he heard of the disaster he realized that there was nothing he could do to reverse the result, so headed back to Bohemia to secure the northern border of his own kingdom. He had already ensured that his key cities were adequately fortified and that monasteries were turned into strongholds to provide places of refuge for their local populations. On the basis of these precautions alone Czech legends would later claim that King Wenceslaus I of Bohemia saved Western Europe, but the Mongols were more hindered by the natural barrier of mountains than Bohemian castles. They consequently moved further east and entered Moravia. There are no records of the Mongols seizing any fortified places in Moravia and it is a plausible argument that they did not even try to do so, since they were in a hurry and may have completed the journey through Moravia in only one day and a night. Nevertheless, the passage of the Mongols inflicted some damage upon the countryside. In 1247 a charter would be issued to the city of Opava guaranteeing economic privileges based on certain non-specified local destruction by the Mongols, but Moravia was nowhere seriously depopulated as some parts of the Kingdom of Hungary would be, and its towns and other fortified places remained untouched. The Mongols finally entered the Kingdom of Hungary through the Hrozenkov Pass near Trenčín around 21 April. By then the battle of Muhi had taken place, and no doubt the commanders congratulated each other on the two great military victories they had separately achieved.

The figure of a defeated Mongol lies beneath the feet of Duke Henry II on this copy of his tomb in the Museum of the Battle of Legnica. It is there to indicate a moral victory for the Christian army in spite of the military defeat.

Muhi

1241

BACKGROUND TO BATTLE

The likelihood of a Mongol invasion of Hungary was discussed very seriously at a council of war held at Esztergom in late 1240 where King Béla IV of Hungary argued for his preferred strategy, which was to place a natural and easily defensible obstacle between the Hungarians and the Mongols. The problem with that scheme was that the sole natural barrier of any significance was the Danube River, which would have meant leaving open to devastation those parts of his kingdom that lay east of the river. It was not a course of action that appealed to the landowning Hungarian nobility, who urged their king instead to engage in war with the invaders. Any military considerations that lay behind this suggestion were no doubt influenced by the lingering distrust that existed between the king and his lords who, among other areas of disagreement, had been dissatisfied with Béla's recent political reforms and had opposed the welcome he had shown to the Cumans. In the end the barons' counsel prevailed, with disastrous consequences.

Thomas of Split tells us that when rumours of a Mongol invasion reached the ears of the ordinary people of Hungary they treated it as a joke, mainly because they had heard such notions before and nothing had ever materialized. They also had great faith in their king's armed forces. That was a confidence which Thomas of Split did not share; he believed that the lords of Hungary had grown lazy, weak and idle (HBS: 255). King Béla IV took the initiative in spite of the opposition his views had aroused and ordered the fortification of likely entry points around Hungary's borders in the Carpathians. Other steps were taken at a more local level, because recent archaeological work has shown that several churches had last-minute earthwork defences dug around them at this time. Sites that were previously thought to be church graveyards

have now been identified as improvised ditch-work fortifications surrounding ecclesiastical buildings.

Sometime around Christmas Day 1240 the news reached King Béla IV that the Mongols had begun devastating the confines of Hungary adjacent to its borders with Ruś, seizing plunder but without inflicting great physical harm on the population (ESL: 157). As the invaders began to spread around the country they sent scouts on a long way ahead, some probing as far as the Danube. These light horsemen haughtily demonstrated the freedom they had to roam through enemy territory by riding up to any Hungarian knights they encountered and taunting their opponents to join battle with them (HBS: 261). Squads of chosen knights were eventually sent out to fight, but the Mongol horsemen would then simply ride off, loosing arrows as they went. One leader who responded was Ugrin Csák, archbishop of Kalocsa, whom the Mongols lured away from the comparative safety of Pest into a swampy area from which he barely escaped with his life (ESL: 169).

The Sajó River as viewed from the south-eastern riverbank. Both sides of the river were covered by woodland, which meant that the Mongol army could not be seen by the approaching Hungarians. The battlefield at Muhi lies in what is still a rural area.

1 The Mongol main body along with its baggage train take up position away from the Sajó River, probably at the site of the hill of Strázsahalom.

2 Drawn on by Mongol advance units, the army of King Béla IV arrives at the Sajó.

3 The Hungarian army sets up a laager around its camp.

4 Units of the Hungarian army attack Mongols who have already crossed the bridge over the Sajó.

5 The Mongols bring up catapults and bombard the guards.

6 A crossing of the Sajó is made downstream.

7 Another crossing of the Sajó is likely to have been made upstream.

8 The Mongols advance on the Hungarian camp and set fire to tents and wagons.

9 The Mongols attack, leaving a conspicuous gap through which the Hungarians flee.

10 The fleeing Hungarians are caught in swampy ground and massacred.

11 King Béla IV and his supporters flee and head for Croatia.

Battlefield environment

The battle of Muhi was fought around and across the Sajó River, which joins the Takta River before its confluence with the Tisza River. The focal point of the battle was a bridge that took an important medieval roadway through the settlement of Muhi and across the Sajó, which nowadays is muddy and meandering with sandy riverbanks. The battlefield lies in what is still a very flat rural area, and the narrow minor road that crosses the Sajó does so not via a bridge but by means of a chain ferry at a point where the two riverbanks are close together. This may be the site of the famous bridge, although its precise location has yet to be identified. Recent archaeological investigations have established the existence of a former medieval village nearby called Hidvég, the name of which literally means 'the end of the bridge', and research is currently under way to find any wooden structures in the Sajó that may be old bridge supports (Pow & Laszlovszky 2019: 264).

Both the immediate sides of the Sajó are covered in trees along the river's floodplain, which fits in with the descriptions of the Mongol army being concealed from view, although it is more than likely that the width and direction of flow of the river has changed considerably over the centuries. The land is flat all around, including the area where most of the fighting probably took place. This would have been around the site of the Hungarian camp to the east and south of the river, which must be somewhere near the modern battle memorial (Laszlovszky *et al.*2016: 35).

One curious feature of Thomas of Split's narrative is his statement that the Mongol leader Batu ascended a hill in order to spy out carefully his enemies' dispositions (HBS: 263). This is in line with the behaviour of other Mongol commanders at different battles, where the ascent of a hill had religious and symbolic connotations. It is, however, a confusing passage because there is no obvious hill anywhere near the Muhi battle site. Batu's observations must have been conducted

east of the river, so it may be that mounds existed there in 1241 but have since disappeared under the plough. The Hungarian campfires would have been visible from several kilometres away, however, so Batu's observations could have been made from the location of the Mongol camp, which, for security reasons, must have been a considerable distance from the fighting. The most likely candidate is a hill called Strázsahalom that appears on old maps. The hill's name means 'a place used for military reconnaissance' and may have been the highest point in the entire region before modern agriculture changed its appearance. The site is 11km (6.8 miles) from the Sajó River (Pow & Laszlovszky 2019: 281).

The narrow minor road that now crosses the Sajó River does so not by a bridge but by means of a chain ferry located at a point where the two riverbanks are close together. This may be the site of the famous bridge, although the precise location of the crossing has yet to be identified.

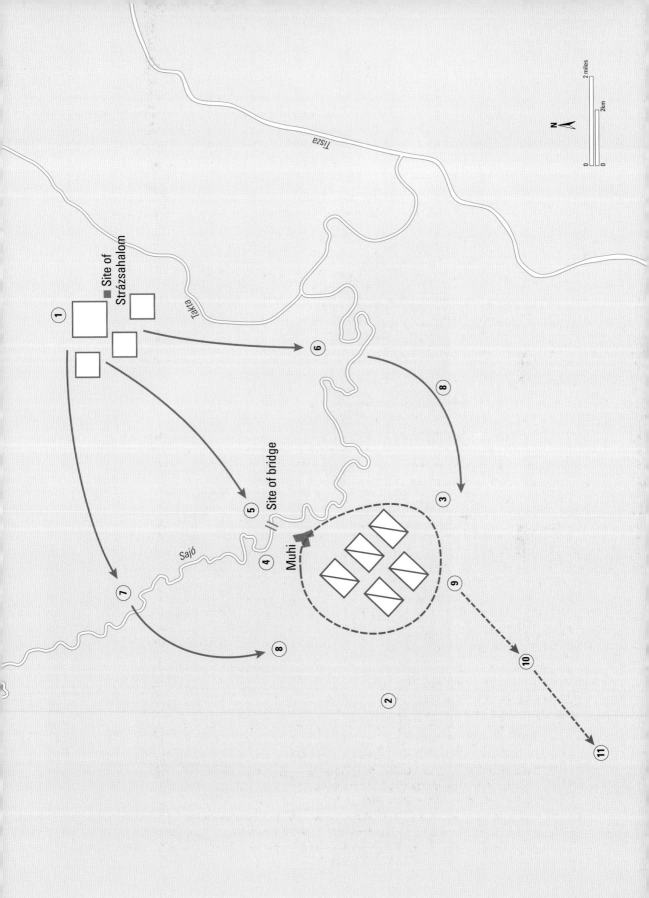

Site of Strázsahalom

Tisza

Takta

Site of bridge

Sajó

Muhi

2 miles

2km

N

INTO COMBAT

All three primary sources are broadly in agreement when it comes to the overall course of the battle of Muhi from the time when the Hungarians left the Danube. The first encounters with the invaders had been made somewhere to the east of Pest, and Thomas of Split sensibly suggests that these skirmishes were part of a strategic feigned retreat designed to lure the Hungarian army as far away as possible from its strongest defences. In addition to being enticed away *from* safety, however, they were also being conducted *towards* the Mongol main body, out of which the advanced troops had emerged. If so the strategy

Ugrin (or Ugolin) Csák, who served as archbishop of Kalocsa from 1219 until his death at the battle of Muhi in 1241, is represented by this 2000 statue by Csilla Halassy. Ugrin, who narrowly escaped death in a swamp near Pest, would be killed when the Hungarians' attempted flight out of the defended camp led to a marsh. (uploader/ Wikimedia/Public Domain)

was completely successful, because King Béla IV set off with his entire army in pursuit of a mysterious and elusive quarry.

To the sceptical Hungarian nobles the Mongols' withdrawal confirmed their views that the invaders were no serious threat and that the king's behaviour was not cautious but cowardly. Some optimistic knights even began to suggest that the retreating Mongols had abandoned Hungary altogether in the face of the Hungarians' brave advance. The sobering reality was provided when Béla's army reached the Sajó River and its bridge. Realizing that some of the Mongol army were encamped across the river (even though most of their forces were concealed from view by woodland) the Hungarians prudently set up a position with the river in front of them.

In all likelihood the Mongol host had been camped there for some time with their herds, wagons and camp-followers stationed far to the rear. Batu had selected the position as his preferred battlefield, and the Hungarians were now most obligingly advancing towards it. Béla reckoned that the bridge over the Sajó was the only possible crossing point because the river was wide and muddy (ESL: 181). For additional protection the king ordered that the Hungarians' tents should be pitched close together and enclosed within a laager of carts and shields. The sceptical Thomas of Split, who was of course aware of the tragic outcome, likens the ensuing situation to the army being confined in a pen or caught in a net, a position made more awkward by entangled tent ropes running across each other and making it impossible to move freely within the trap the Hungarians had unintentionally made for themselves (HBS: 261–63).

The fields north of the Sajó River where the Mongol armies lay in wait for the Hungarians. No fighting took place on that side of the river. Somewhere behind this viewpoint the Mongol leader Batu ascended a hill in order to spy out carefully his enemies' dispositions.

Ugrin Csák, Archbishop of Kalocsa

One remarkable feature of the Hungarian campaign is the participation of several fighting bishops and archbishops. Thomas of Split tells us (HBS: 257) that these belligerent senior clergymen were never content to maintain modest households as would have been more appropriate for senior churchmen, but possessed great wealth and were accustomed to leading companies of other knights into battle. The outstanding example is provided by Ugrin (or Ugolin) Csák, who served as archbishop of Kalocsa from 1219 until his death at the battle of Muhi in 1241. He had fought in the Fifth Crusade two years before his consecration when he accompanied King Andrew II of Hungary (to whom he may have been closely related) in the Holy Land as part of what is believed to have been the largest royal army ever to participate in a crusade (ESL: 187). Ugrin is recorded as having founded a hospital in Kalocsa after being installed as archbishop, but the main preoccupation for him and his fellow Hungarian bishops was the prosecution of war against heretics in Bosnia, although Ugrin does not appear to have served there in any personal military capacity. When the Mongols arrived in Hungary he and his fellow bishops faced up to the new threat with the greatest zeal, although Master Roger implies that Ugrin had originally been planning to flee, having ordered galleys from Venice for himself and his colleagues (ESL: 157). If so, he had a rapid change of heart and became one of the first military leaders in Hungary to confront the Mongols. The incident happened when Batu moved against Pest and then withdrew to entice the Hungarian king to attack him. Ugrin pursued a Mongol detachment across marshy ground. The lighter Mongol archers crossed the swamp with ease, but the heavier knights became bogged down, at which the Mongols launched volleys of arrows at them, killing all but four of Ugrin's companions. The archbishop escaped and returned to Pest in great embarrassment (ESL: 169).

Ugrin met his death at the battle of Muhi, where he criticized King Béla IV for his dilatoriness in confronting the Mongols. When Ugrin attacked the Mongols his opponents reportedly cried out and fled from him as if he were a bolt of lightning (HBS: 265). Most ironically, Ugrin, who had narrowly escaped death in a swamp near Pest, was killed when the Hungarians' attempted flight out of the defended camp also led to a marsh (HBS: 269). Archbishop Ugrin Csák is remembered to this day in Kalocsa, where a fine modern statue of him now stands.

Batu Khan

Master Roger refers to the Mongol leader as a king of kings and a lord of the Tatars and names him as Batu (ESL: 163), thus correctly identifying the overall leader of the operation. Batu was the son of Jochi and a grandson of Chinggis (Genghis) Khan. Master Roger, who suffered personally from Batu's military acumen and ruthless cruelty, notes later that Batu began to burn down villages and slaughtered everyone regardless of sex or age (ESL: 169). Other chroniclers too noted his thoroughness of destruction. When Batu took the city of Kozel'sk in May 1238 he ordered his troops to slaughter everyone, sparing neither children nor infants nursing at their mothers' breasts (GVC: 43).

This fierce reputation may well have contributed to the fact that when his father Jochi died in 1225 his elder brother Orda had agreed that Batu should succeed their father, and when Chinggis Khan died in 1227 Jochi's lands were divided between the two brothers with Batu taking over the western part and Orda the eastern part. At the great Mongol meeting of 1235 Ögedei ordered Batu to conduct military operations further west. This was the operation that moved successfully against the cities of Ruś in 1237. When the Cumans fled to the safety of King Béla IV, Batu sent no fewer than four demands for them to be returned and was infuriated by the Hungarian king's defiance. With the loyal support of Sübe'etei, Batu led the assault on Hungary and triumphed at Muhi.

Leaving others to pursue the fleeing Hungarian king, Batu withdrew through Transylvania to secure possession of conquered Ruś now that no Hungarian advance could threaten it. On arriving at the Volga delta, Batu set up his headquarters at Sarai, which became the capital of that part of the Mongol empire that became known as the Golden Horde, the power that was to control Russia for more than two centuries. The adjective 'golden' is supposed to refer to the magnificence of Batu Khan's headquarters camp. Batu claimed sovereignty over the whole of Ruś, the princes of which paid him tribute in money and military support but otherwise suffered little interference in their own principalities provided that they cooperated with the Mongols. The Golden Horde eventually controlled a region extending from Central Asia to the Dnieper River in what are now Ukraine, Russia and Kazakhstan from 1242 until 1480, and it was in the form of the Golden Horde that the Mongols would attack Poland and Hungary again later in the 13th century. Batu died in 1255 having laid strong foundations, and of all the Khanates the Golden Horde ruled its territories for the longest period of time, even outlasting the Yuan (Mongol) dynasty of China.

At this point, Thomas of Split tells us, Batu ordered his troops to seize the bridge over the Sajó. That was the beginning of the battle of Muhi on 11 April 1241, two days after the battle of Liegnitz. Fortunately for the Hungarians, someone from the Mongol side (probably a captive pressed into service) informed Béla of the plan, at which King Kálmán of Galicia and Archbishop Ugrin roused their own contingents and went to the bridge sometime around midnight. They quickly discovered that some of the Mongols had already crossed, at which point the Hungarians units attacked them, killing a great number (HBS: 263). *Yuan shi* adds that there was a senior casualty on the Mongol side at the bridge, namely Batu's subordinate general Ba'atur. Complaints were made later that Sübe'etei arrived too late to rescue his comrades and that this led to the death of Ba'atur, but Sübe'etei asserted that it was not his fault (YS: 67). The *Tartar Relation* has its own account of the same incident (TR: 82), whereby someone its author describes as the chief general of the Tartars at the bridge was thrown to his death in the depths of the river along with his horse and weapons. The deed, says the *Tartar Relation*, was performed by no less a person than King Kálmán during the first onslaught (TR: 82).

Encouraged by this victory the more complacent elements among the Hungarian knights settled down for the night and went to sleep without

OPPOSITE
A model of the Hungarian laager that provided the defence for King Béla IV's army at Muhi. The model is in the museum of Boldogkő castle in northern Hungary, which was rebuilt after the Mongol invasion.

a care in the world – until the Mongols brought up seven siege catapults and started bombarding the defenders whom the Hungarians had stationed beside the bridge. They fled back to the camp to raise the alarm. With the guards put to flight the Mongols could cross the river easily, although they did not use the bridge alone. In what was to prove a decisive move in the battle at least one separate detachment crossed by a ford downstream from the bridge. To Master Roger they cross by 'a ford' (ESL: 183) and in *Yuan shi* they simply cross downstream (YS: 66), but there may well have been another advance across the river upstream because Thomas of Split refers to 'fords' in the plural (HBS: 263).

This tactic may have been due to Mongol disquiet as to how the battle was going following the loss of Ba'atur at the bridge. Even after crossing the bridge the Mongol leaders were discouraged by the numbers of the enemy and expressed to Sübe'etei their desire to withdraw, arguing among themselves about the course of action. The very short third version of Sübe'etei's biography, produced as a temple inscription in 1286, contains a highly revealing phrase stating that when the main force joined in they discovered that things were not going well (YS: 40). Fortunately for the Mongols, Sübe'etei ordered this army to the lower reaches of the river to cross and attack the camp directly, resulting in a Mongol victory (YS: 66).

The Chinese account therefore suggests that the fording of the Sajó downstream was made out of desperation on the Mongols' part, but it had a successful outcome because when dawn broke a huge host of Mongols began to encircle the Hungarian camp. Thomas of Split is again scornful of the Hungarian response, because when the guards from the bridge arrived back in camp and told their comrades about what had happened the majority of the knights displayed no great concern. Instead of immediately grabbing their weapons and mounting their horses they rose slowly from their beds, combed their hair and washed in no great hurry. This casual approach was not shared by King Kálmán and Archbishop Ugrin, however, whose detachments had already fought the Mongols at the bridge. They set off to renew the battle along with Rembald de Voczon, Master of the Templars. Like the archbishop the Templars, notes Thomas of Split approvingly, behaved as proper soldiers should and had been alert and on their guard all night. The Latin knights (the Templars in Hungary were mostly French) are recorded as having made a great slaughter of the enemy (HBS: 267). Again, there is likely to have been a sizeable presence from men who worked the Templars' lands.

Other combatants on the Hungarian side now moved forward and engaged the enemy who surrounded them but, overwhelmed by the numbers, they soon withdrew to the camp, where Archbishop Ugrin upbraided King Béla IV for his negligence and his slowness to respond. Some of the Hungarian army then followed Archbishop Ugrin back into battle, but many others were paralysed with fear and did not know how to respond. Kálmán, Ugrin and Voczon again took the lead and launched themselves back into the hand-to-hand fighting. The Templar Master was killed during this stage of the action and the other two leaders were seriously wounded (HBS: 265). With no effective military response

emerging from within the Hungarian camp the gleeful Mongol host were able to surround their targets completely and pressed forward their attack at leisure. To increase the confusion they set fire to wagons and tents at various points around the perimeter of the camp and accompanied the process with typically dense volleys of arrows. This was followed by hand-to-hand encounters, stabbing their victims with spears when they were at close quarters.

The Hungarian mindset had now shifted completely to flight, but regardless of the fact that they were surrounded they had already made things difficult for themselves within the laager, so that one man trampled upon another over the guy ropes of the tents and as many were injured thus as were by the arrows. At this point the Mongols launched a catapult bombardment directly on to the camp until many of the Hungarian tents and field fortifications were wrecked. They then prepared very conspicuously for a mass charge, and here another good example of classic Mongol tactics came into its own, because Sübe'etei had not completely surrounded the Hungarian camp. He realized that a cornered enemy would fight to the death, so he had left an obvious escape route. Thomas of Split likens the action to leaving open a door which led to ground of the Mongols' own choosing.

At first only a handful of horsemen took advantage of the prominent gap that led to apparent safety, but once panic spread armour and weapons were discarded as a human flood began to escape from the wrecked Hungarian camp. The Mongols followed them cautiously, their fleeing victims' paths being marked by their discarded valuables, which the

The Sajó River at almost its narrowest point upstream from the bridge. A Mongol crossing may have been made near here, possibly due to Mongol disquiet as to how the battle of Muhi was going following the loss of the Mongol general Ba'atur at the bridge.

The Muhi battlefield, looking away from the memorial. This area, which is now crossed by a modern road, would have seen the fiercest fighting of the battle and the beginning of the Mongols' relentless pursuit.

Mongols ignored for the time being. The main body of the Mongols calmly let the frightened men run through their ranks, and when the Hungarians were exhausted a further session of very one-sided hand-to-hand combat began. Thomas of Split notes swords and spears predominating as the helpless victims were cut down or were left to be hunted down afterwards by the light horsemen, who brought down the fugitives as if the riders had been on a hunting expedition back in Mongolia. Matters were made worse because the convenient gap in the Mongol lines ultimately led to a marsh and many were drowned there, including the brave Archbishop Ugrin of Kalocsa, Archbishop Matthias of Esztergom and Bishop Gregory of Győr (HBS: 269–71).

The days that immediately followed the battle produced scenes of unmitigated horror. Thomas of Split would note that the land was strewn with corpses for two days' journey around and that the ground was stained by blood. Some victims were still alive hours after the battle; others lay moving in death, swollen like inflated wineskins. Some tried to escape by smearing themselves with blood and hiding among the dead, but the Mongols were not fooled and accompanied this particular round of execution with the killing of other prisoners; a task, according to Thomas of Split, in which the Mongol women willingly joined. Further psychological and deceptive warfare occurred shortly afterwards when the Mongols took over the camp and found the great seal of the Hungarian chancellor. With it they issued false proclamations in his name telling the inhabitants not to fear the Mongols but to stay in their houses. Unprotected and largely unarmed, they became easy prey.

Esztergom and Székesfehérvár

1242

BACKGROUND TO BATTLE

The encounters in Hungary that followed the battle of Muhi were very different in nature from the largely one-sided Mongol victory across the Sajó River, which is regarded as one of the greatest achievements and fiercest battles in their history (Laszlovszky *et al.* 2016: 30). I have chosen to concentrate on the first two sieges - Esztergom and Székesfehérvár – for which there is the most material, but they should be regarded as typical of the action at the four instances of resistance, all of which were characterized by desperate defence and ultimate victory. Every encounter also included important contributions from visiting Western European knights.

Following the battle of Muhi King Béla IV fled first to the Duchy of Austria, where he was not well received. Instead, Duke Frederick II detained him until the wretched monarch agreed to repay an outstanding loan. The debt was settled by the king pawning three Hungarian counties and, in an astonishing lack of sympathy for the monarch who had done his best to save Eastern Europe from the Mongols, the Austrian troops moved into their new acquisitions and began to plunder neighbouring areas until the Hungarians drove them back (HBS: 273). King Béla IV's brother Kálmán had also fled from the battlefield and was pursued as far as Pest, where he found many Hungarians who had already gone there for refuge when they heard the outcome of the battle of Muhi. Kálmán was sceptical of Pest's defences and urged the refugees to move on again. When they refused to listen to his pleas he abandoned them and went on his way across the Drava River. Kálmán eventually died in June 1241 from the wounds he received at Muhi.

Left to their own devices the inhabitants of Pest decided to make a stand with the Drava to their backs and constructed what fortifications they could against a Mongol attack that would be launched overland. The process involved creating wicker barricades filled with earth and digging ditches, but sometime towards the end of April 1241 the Mongols were upon them before the rudimentary defences were completed. It is in Thomas of Split's chronicle that we find the first references to arrows being exchanged between knights and Mongols across a fortified barrier, as would soon happen at Esztergom, because the Mongols attacked Pest from all sides with intense archery fire, to which the defenders responded with arrows, crossbow bolts and stones hurled from catapults. According to Thomas of Split, however, the Mongol arrows never failed to hit their mark and no breastplate, shield or armour was proof against them, so Pest fell after two or three days of fierce fighting. The Mongols had now secured the left bank of the Danube (HBS: 275).

The areas of Hungary that lay to the east of Pest and its natural river barrier would remain wholly under Mongol control from April 1241 to April 1242, and most of the spring and summer of 1241 would see the Mongols plundering and enslaving their defeated foes. To intimidate the Hungarians who were sheltering on the far bank of the Danube the Mongols piled up the dead bodies of their victims beside the river at locations where they could be clearly seen by anyone who was reconnoitring (HBS: 278–79).

Meanwhile King Béla IV had reached Zagreb in the course of his flight, from where he sent a letter dated 18 May 1241 to Pope Gregory IX requesting urgent help (HBS: 280). This was the first of several similar pleas despatched by Béla (or others on his behalf) over the ensuing months. Duke Frederick II wrote a letter to Rome on 20 June and another to his fellow European monarchs on 3 July 1241 calling for a common response under imperial leadership. Some welcome spiritual (if not military) help was forthcoming when the Pope placed Béla and Kálmán under the protection of Rome and assured anyone who joined a crusade against the Mongols that they would receive the same spiritual rewards in the form of the indulgences that

King Béla IV's brother Kálmán, depicted in this 1931 statue in Gödöllö, Hungary, fled from the battlefield of Muhi and was pursued as far as Pest. He died in June of the same year from the wounds he received at Muhi. He is supposed to have killed the Mongol general Ba'atur during the first onslaught. (Bcs78/Wikimedia/ CC BY-SA 3.0)

were customarily granted to anyone who fought in the Holy Land (Jackson 2005: 65). The situation was obviously being taken seriously, and in the current climate anything could be believed. Many feared that the Mongols might even be intending to make for Rome, devastating all in their path. Preparing for the worst, Béla ordered that the body of St Stephen should be removed from Székesfehérvár and taken to the castle of Klis on the Adriatic coast near to Split, where the saint's relics and various treasures were shut up for safety along with some members of Béla's immediate family (HBS: 286–87).

In spite of all the pleas that emanated from Eastern Europe and the prayers that were sent back from Rome in reply, no military help was despatched to complement the pious encouragement, so Béla made a third desperate appeal to whoever would become the new Pope (the Papal chair would be vacant until June 1243) in an important letter dated 19 January 1242. It described the soldiers of Hungary as a wall for the Lord's house and as Christian heroes who had held the line of the Danube which the Lord had so far prevented the Mongols from crossing. The letter then requested a crusade to be preached among the Venetians in particular because of the Hungarians' need for their *ballistarii* (Sinor 1999: 17). In antiquity the word *ballistarii* had indicated the operators of some form of catapult or siege engines for throwing stones (*ballista*), but by the 13th century a customary distinction was made between such machines and handheld crossbows, which were the weapons sought by the letter (Turnbull 2009: 312–14). The only reply Béla received was a sympathetic letter from the Curia, but even if no Venetian crossbowmen arrived, it was noted above that crossbows had been present at Liegnitz and Pest, and the highly valued weapons were soon to play a part in the defence of Esztergom.

The Mongol invasion of Hungary as imagined in the *Chronica Hungarorum*, a work dating from 1486 by the Hungarian historian János Thuróczy, aka Johannes de Thurocz. After the battle of Muhi, the Mongols dragged enslaved Hungarians away, but in this depiction the Mongols are shown as Muslims. (Johannes de Thurocz/Wikimedia/Public Domain

The sieges of Esztergom and Székesfehérvár, 1242

1 Having crossed the frozen Danube, the Mongols divide their forces: one division goes south in pursuit of King Béla IV while the other heads for Esztergom overland.

2 The Mongols destroy the outer defence of Esztergom using catapults and the rich burghers abandon the lower part of the settlement.

3 The Mongols attack the citadel, which is defended by crossbowmen.

4 The Mongols leave Esztergom and advance to Székesfehérvár.

Battlefield environment

According to Master Roger, Esztergom surpassed every other city in Hungary. It had been the country's first royal residence and provided probably its first bishopric, so it would represent a major prize for the Mongols. Esztergom was built on a bend in the Danube and its citadel, the place of last stand, towered high above the city upon an impressive bluff. It may well have involved stone and is still an impressive sight today, but in 1242 the lower defences of the city were predominantly of wood and comparatively weak.

The key to King Béla IV's preferred strategy had always been the Danube, the river that under normal circumstances provided a formidable obstacle and a scenario that the Mongol armies typically preferred to avoid. Indeed, as flimsy Pest had shown, the Danube provided the only real barrier to the Mongol advance, and the defensive potential of even narrow stretches of water had been demonstrated at Wrocław where an island had provided a refuge. Unfortunately for the Hungarians, the winter of 1241/42 was unusually severe and the Danube had frozen over, leaving Esztergom open to assault overland, but the Mongol ravages east of the Danube in 1241 had also been made easier by the absence of strong fortresses, because the Hungarians owned little in the way of castles. Most Hungarian strongpoints had only beaten-earth walls, and any castles built of stone were in the west on the border with Austria. This factor provided a clue as to the Hungarians' future strategy, because encouraging hints had already been given that the Mongols had a weakness when it came to anything involving stone walls. We noted earlier that the only survivors at Kraków had locked themselves inside a fortified stone church. That instance was far from a victory over the Mongols, but it was a small pointer towards what could be achieved with strong defences; and another encouraging factor was the knowledge that three years earlier the largely wooden walls of the cities of Ruś as well had not all been mere pushovers. Torzhok had withstood battering rams for two weeks (CN: 82–83), while Kozel'sk had held out for seven weeks. During their last stand the townspeople of Kozel'sk sallied out, destroyed the Mongol catapults and inflicted 4,000 casualties on the besiegers (GVC: 46–47). Pest's more rudimentary fortifications had been swept to one side. Would Esztergom fare any better?

Esztergom (Gran) had been Hungary's first royal residence and provided probably its first bishopric, so it represented a major target for the Mongols. Esztergom was built on a bend in the Danube and its citadel, the place of last stand, towered high above the city upon an impressive bluff. (Batomi/Wikimedia/ CC BY-SA 3.0)

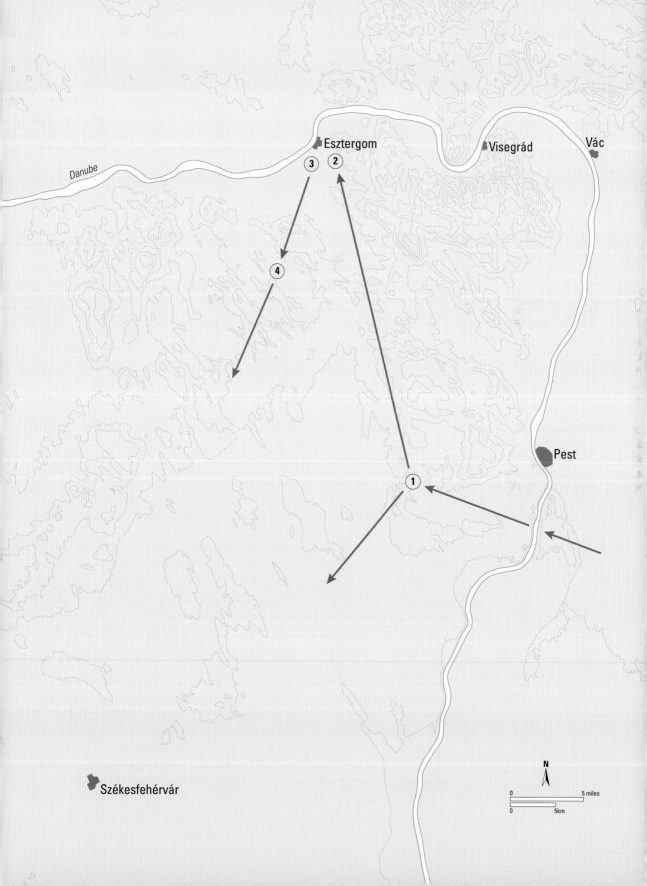

Danube

Esztergom

③ ②

Visegrád

Vác

④

Pest

①

Székesfehérvár

N

0   5 miles

0   5km

INTO COMBAT

Thomas's account of the siege of Esztergom is surprisingly brief. He simply notes (HBS: 289) the Mongols crossing the frozen Danube in pursuit of the fleeing King Béla IV and then besieging the city, at which the Mongols soon captured it and set the buildings on fire, slaughtering the inhabitants but gaining little in the way of plunder because the Hungarians had moved all of their possessions to the citadel. This is a reasonable summary of the events, but it plays down the fact that the high fortress or citadel of Esztergom held out and provided the Mongols with their first proper reversal in Hungary, a setback that was to be repeated at least three more times before the conquerors withdrew.

As noted earlier, the great cities of western Hungary such as Esztergom were first of all protected by the waters of the Danube. In order to keep their natural barrier secure during the severe winter of 1241/42 the Hungarians broke the ice cover every morning while foot soldiers fought desperate skirmishes across the surface against Mongol raiding parties, but one day the frost was so severe that the river had frozen to an unbreakable depth. The Mongols, whose scouts were watching from a distance, suspected that this may have happened and decided to test the theory by leaving some unguarded horses on the far side of the river for three days. Thinking that the enemy had departed, the Hungarian defenders crossed the ice and captured the animals, thus revealing to the Mongols that a safe crossing was now possible.

The precise location of the subsequent passage of the ice by the Mongol army is unknown but was probably somewhere immediately south of Pest, and according to Thomas of Split it happened sometime after the end of January 1242. Master Roger gives no date for the crossing, but there is a persistent folk tradition that it took place on Christmas Day 1241. There may have been a minor encounter then because Master Roger notes much skirmishing taking place over a longer period of time, but early February must be the date for the main crossing because in Béla's letter of 19 January noted earlier the river is still providing a secure barrier.

Having crossed the river the Mongols divided their army in two. One division continued south in pursuit of the fugitive Béla; the other prepared for a siege of Esztergom, which the triumphant Mongols were able to approach overland. While they were still a safe distance away their engineers assembled 30 siege engines. For their part the Hungarian defenders strengthened Esztergom's existing fortifications with moats, walls and wooden towers and were so self-confident at what they had achieved that they felt they could take on the whole world (ESL: 215–17).

The fact that the attack on Esztergom was launched overland rather than across the river is confirmed by Master Roger's reference to the Mongols forcing prisoners to build walls from brushwood outside the moat. The Mongols then hurled stones from behind these defences day and night and completely demolished the wooden towers which the citizens had rapidly erected. The stones were then exchanged for bags of earth and the Mongol catapults began to rain these down to fill up the moat, which we must presume was a dry one. None of the defenders dared appear on the brow of the ditch to challenge them because of covering fire provided in the form of Mongol arrows and stones.

The largely wooden fortifications at Esztergom and Székesfehérvár (Stuhlweißenburg) would have resembled the wooden walls and towers shown in this painting of a *veche* (assembly of citizens) in Pskov. (Apollinary Vasnetsov/ Wikimedia/Public Domain)

Faced by this terrifying onslaught the richer burghers of Esztergom took matters into their own hands. In a zeal to protect their own properties they set fire to the wooden houses of the commoners below their own fine palaces and used the flames as a way of destroying anything they could not carry to safety, burning expensive cloth and garments, slaughtering their horses and burying gold and silver in the ground. The attacking Mongols realized that these deliberate acts of destruction would deprive them of plunder, so once the moat was secured they constructed a stout palisade around Esztergom and killed anyone trying to leave. The Mongols then marched through their own palisade in an orderly fashion and attacked the rich citizens' palaces and mansions, leaving, according to Master Roger, only 15 people alive and torturing any captives they took, presumably so that they would disclose their hiding places for treasure. Even grand ladies who tried to surrender were killed. This stage of the siege has been confirmed by archaeological investigation, because a human skeleton was unearthed under the charred beams of a building in Esztergom alongside highly valuable metal objects dated to the 13th century. The dead person's body was found in a storage pit (Gyucha *et al.* 2019: 1044–55).

After this the Mongols moved against the citadel on the hill which still stood defiantly above them, and this was where the fiercest hand-to-hand fighting took place between the Mongols and the European knights. The high castle of Esztergom was under the command of someone whom Roger refers to as a Spaniard called Simon, a knight who had command of many crossbowmen (ESL: 218–19). This Simon was the brother of Constance of Aragon, who had married King Emeric of Hungary (r. 1196–1204) in 1198. Simon had followed his sister to Esztergom and married into the Hungarian nobility.

Master Roger's account of the Mongol attack on Esztergom ends abruptly with the mention of Simon and his manful defence, but in the end the citadel of Esztergom held out and the Mongols withdrew defeated.

Two views of a crossbow nut dating from before 1272. Weighing 8g and with a diameter of 2.9cm, it is made of staghorn and iron alloy and was found at Haifa, Israel. Crossbows were widely used in warfare throughout Christian Europe during the 13th century and, as in the case of this example, accompanied Western European armies on crusade in the Levant as well as the European settlers in the Crusader states. (metmuseum.org/CC0 1.0)

We may assume that the crossbows were well-used and that numerous single combats took place between armoured Mongols and the defenders with spear, mace and sword, as a different account notes for the defence of Kyiv, where its inhabitants scaled the breached defences and one could witness close combat while the passage of arrows blocked the light from the eyes of the defeated (GVC: 48). The failure at Esztergom seems to have been a disappointing setback for the Mongol invaders. Although the description is garbled, the longer biography of Sübe'etei in *Yuan Shi*, states that the princes and Sübe'etei joined together to capture a city in Hungary on the Danube (which is probably Esztergom) and that they 'returned', which may be a euphemism for 'retreated' (YS: 67).

The Mongols then went on to attack Székesfehérvár (Stuhlweißenburg), which possessed very different natural defences in the form of marshes. The swamplands had of course been frozen solid, allowing the Mongols free rein up until then, but the marshes were now melting rapidly in the thaw (ESL: 219). Thomas of Split adds that Székesfehérvár was defended by a garrison of Latins who had built engines of war to defend it. The term 'Latins' refers to the Knights Hospitaller of St John, whose main seat in Hungary was Székesfehérvár, so once again we see a contingent of Western European chivalry in action on Hungary's behalf, and to add to the achievements of the Templars at Liegnitz and Muhi the Hospitallers drove the Mongols back after much fierce single combat (HBS: 290–91).

More successes would follow, and a third fortress that Master Roger calls the castle of St Martin of Pannonia – in reality Hungary's oldest monastery the Benedictine foundation of Pannonhalma – was valiantly and successfully defended by its Abbot even though it suffered considerable damage (Pow 2019a: 241). Attacks were also made against Veszprém, which was protected by good walls, but Győr (Raab) fell, as did Visegrád, another fortress situated on an imposing hilltop at the Danube Bend. Many smaller settlements suffered worse devastation in relation to their size. In the villages of Tázlár, Csengele and Szank, archaeology has revealed evidence of Mongol massacres such as corpses of victims, weapons and coins dated to the time of the invasion, and there have been many other finds on the sites of abandoned villages and monasteries. For example, the remains of burned palisades have been discovered within the ditch system that was hastily dug to provide defences for the church in the village of Csengele-Fecskés.

Dating from *c.*1250, this catapult projectile was found at Montfort castle, aka Starkenberg, a Teutonic Order stronghold formerly in the kingdom of Jerusalem and now in Israel. Siege warfare was an ever-present threat in the warfare of the 13th century, given the reliance placed upon fortifications throughout Christian Europe and its outposts in the Levant. (Heritage Art/Heritage Images via Getty Images)

Elsewhere the settlement of Orosháza-Bónum appears to have been violently destroyed, because there is evidence for extensive burning inconsistent with normal domestic life such as thick layers of ash, and the dating fits a Mongol surprise attack on the village. Human skeletal remains were also found there; a child's body retained in death the tip of a short sword or dagger. One fragmentary adult leg bone displayed multiple marks of cuts, and all these features date to the final phase of the village's existence, suggesting that the Mongols had destroyed it once and for all. Similarly, excavations at the site of the village of Cegléd-Madarászhalom near Pest have revealed the remains of a young woman and two children in a burned-out semi-subterranean structure along with a variety of tools and coins dating from the time of Béla IV. The victims' door had been barricaded against entry, so presumably the attacking Mongols set the place on fire. At another site a mace head has been discovered which has been associated with the Mongol raiders (Gyucha *et al.* 2019: 1044–55). All the draught animals had been seized by the Mongols, so in the aftermath of the invasion peasants desperately yoked themselves to ploughs in an attempt to resume planting (Laszlovszky *et al.* 2018: 433).

We must not, however, think that the Mongols left Hungary with their armies totally unscathed. John of Plano Carpini refers (HM: 43) to the existence of two important cemeteries in the Tartar country: one for their

Hospitallers face the Mongols at Székesfehérvár, 1242

Following their repulse from Esztergom, the Mongols are attacking the walls of Székesfehérvár. This section of the defences is being held by a contingent of Knights of St John dressed in their characteristic dark robes, an encumbrance when on crusade in the Levant but very welcome in the harsh Hungarian winter. Crossbowmen are also in action and doing deadly work against the Mongols, whose heavy cavalrymen are being used for the hand-to-hand combat of the siege rather than the lightly armoured archers, who keep up a barrage of arrows from a distance. The battered wooden walls of Székesfehérvár are covered with frozen snow and ice, but the marshes that surround Székesfehérvár are beginning to melt into mud, so the fighting is a desperate race against time.

nobility and a separate one for those killed in Hungary, where there had been many casualties. Indeed, many local oral traditions and associated folklore in areas linked to the Mongol incursions are remarkably upbeat, ignoring the fear and devastation and stressing instead the villagers' bravery and cunning in outwitting the Tartar hordes. For example, persistent oral traditions include tales of people hiding in the swamplands and escaping from their pursuers, or even misleading the Mongols by placing pumpkins on poles to make the raiders think that the village was defended by an army. Basic defensive measures include hiding old pots in the swamps with their open mouths just below the water level to damage the Mongol horses' legs. Other tricks included baking a fresh loaf of bread and placing it on the castle wall to indicate that the inhabitants had sufficient food to withstand a siege.

Following their orgy of destruction the Mongol forces made their famous and mysterious withdrawal from Hungary. The Mongol sources provide no explanation for the abrupt departure, and many historians for a long time believed that the withdrawal was due to the death of Ögedei Khan in December 1241. Batu was therefore forced to halt operations and return to Mongolia to help elect the new khan, a decision that is traditionally regarded as having saved Europe. In fact Batu never went back to Mongolia, and instead remained in the southern Russian steppes where he consolidated his position as ruler of the Golden Horde. There are, however, other theories as to why the Mongols left so abruptly. It has been suggested that it was an acknowledgement of the Mongols' unease about facing castles, and in recent years a lively debate had been conducted as to whether the withdrawal was brought about by climate change on a localized scale, with warm and dry summers during 1238–41 followed by cold and wet conditions in early 1242. Marshy terrain across the Hungarian plain most likely reduced the amount of pastureland and decreased the mobility and effectiveness of the Mongol cavalry, while despoliation and depopulation contributed to widespread famine (Pow 2019b: 315).

If we look at the primary sources, Master Roger writes that instead of travelling directly down the Danube the withdrawing Mongol columns proceeded eastwards into an already devastated Transylvania before moving southwards. This implies that the Mongol forces were not rushing straight back to Mongolia in response to a recently received command. Instead, Master Roger implies that there was a deliberate and slow withdrawal as the Mongols combed through the already devastated lands in search of anything

they had missed when they entered. Finally, the testimony that Batu slowly moved southward into another area of Europe could suggest a shifting of his strategic objectives in early 1242 – maybe even an intended and very optimistic move against Constantinople as a wealthy target. It certainly does not suggest any urgent reaction to the news of Ögedei's death for which Batu felt a pressing need to return to the steppes that same spring (Pow 2021: 13).

One other possible reason for the Mongols' sudden withdrawal from Hungary was simply that, being unable to conquer the major fortresses west of the Danube, the Mongols had turned their full attentions to capturing King Béla IV, because while the main army withdrew another was heading south after the Hungarian king. Learning of their pursuit, Béla had left Zagreb before the Mongols had a chance to cross the Drava and headed for Split, accompanied by a force of Knights Hospitaller (Hunyadi 2004: 41–42). There he was warmly received; but Béla wanted more than a welcome, he wanted a fast galley with which to escape to sea. When none was forthcoming he left Split for the safety of the island of Trogir (Trau) and then moved even further across the Adriatic Sea to the island of Čiovo (HBS: 294–95).

Turning their backs on the Hungarian fortresses the Mongols moved rapidly through Croatia in pursuit of Béla. It may seem surprising that the Mongols went to such lengths to pursue the defeated king. The territory was inhospitable in winter, but it appears that they went there just to punish Béla, and there was much devastation along the way. On the approach to Split the Mongols even slaughtered helpless lepers. They paused outside the walls of Split whose citizens had erected defensive siege engines, but the Mongol high command soon became convinced that Béla was not inside. They were right, but they incorrectly believed him to be holed up in the

The Mongols believed that the fugitive King Béla IV was hiding inside the castle of Klis in the mountains behind Split. Klis became the subject of a fierce assault. The initial attacks up the slopes would probably have been led by forlorn-hope squads impressed from among the captives. The stubborn resistance made the Mongols all the more ferocious and they came right up to Klis's walls for hand-to-hand combat.

The death of Ögedei Khan in 1241 is usually cited as the reason for the Mongol withdrawal from Hungary after the battle of Muhi. (Universal History Archive/ Universal Images Group via Getty Images)

castle of Klis, not Trogir, so this fortress built on a rocky mountain became the latest target for a Mongol attack. Just as at Esztergom, Székesfehérvár and Pannonhalma the steppe horsemen were repulsed, and Thomas of Split takes delight in telling us how they first attacked from horseback, launching arrows and throwing spears. When this had only limited effect they dismounted and began to creep up through the rocks, but the defenders threw down stones upon them and caused many casualties. Judging by previous Mongol campaigns, the initial assaults up the slopes would probably have been led by forlorn-hope squads impressed from among the captives. The stubborn resistance made the Mongols all the more ferocious and they came right up to Klis's walls for hand-to-hand combat. These genuine Mongol warriors must then have broken through Klis's outer defences because they looted houses and took away plunder, but we must assume that when they realized that Béla was not there they did not enter the castle and changed their attack to Trogir.

The citizens of Trogir were much alarmed at the terror displayed by the Hungarian refugees who had found shelter among them. Some of the incomers began to spread rumours that the Mongols possessed large numbers of huge siege machines, or even that they were planning to pile up stones to make a fantastic artificial mountain from which they could assault the walls. The latter belief was probably based on the Mongol technique noted earlier of filling up ditches with brushwood and soil by means of catapult bombardment. Of course, all this prevarication may simply have been a ruse to cover the citizens' own desire to flee to the offshore islands of the Adriatic Sea.

In the event the Mongols took up a position on the seashore, which Béla bravely reconnoitred from a boat. The besiegers then discovered that the land side of Trogir consisted of impassable mudflats, so they withdrew from there as well, and on their way back through Croatia pillaged some less well-defended places. This episode of the Mongol campaign has yielded a legend of a fantasy encounter called the battle of Grobnik, which is not recorded by any contemporary, when thousands of Mongols are supposed to have been killed by Croats. From Croatia the Mongols passed through Bosnia and Serbia, leaving mighty Dubrovnik well alone. Svač (Šas) in Montenegro was among the weakly defended places they encountered, and the massacre there was so extensive that, in Thomas of Split's well-chosen words, '*non reliquentes in eis mingentem ad parietem*' ('they left no one to urinate against a wall') (HBS: 297–303).

Analysis

When the Mongols finally departed from Croatia King Béla IV left his family behind in Klis and returned to Hungary, where a rigorous analysis began of how his kingdom had fared in history's first clash between Mongol warriors and European chivalry. Most of Hungary was devastated, but thanks to the quality of some of its fortresses, the barrier of the Danube and the help of foreign knights, it had survived against all the odds in the face of the most terrible enemies. Nevertheless, the immediate impression given by the Mongol invasion on the ground was one of total destruction, and it was an image that would be long-lasting. Writing even before the attack on Esztergom, a German chronicler claimed somewhat prematurely that the Kingdom of Hungary had been destroyed by the Tartars after having lasted for 350 years (Jackson 2005: 64). Other sources reported that a depleted population meant that fields could not be tilled, and an epidemic in 1243 led to a serious famine that probably claimed more victims than the invasion (Laszlovszky *et al.* 2018: 422–24). The Mongols' political influence beyond Hungary – in Galicia, the eastern frontiers of Poland, Cumania, Bulgaria, and Serbia – would last for over a hundred years in the form of the Golden Horde and, in spite of all the discussion over the mysterious Mongol withdrawal, the Mongols did of course come back (Pow 2019a: 245). Hungary was expecting their return as early as 1247 and Poland was attacked in 1259, as will be described below (Fügedi 1986: 50).

The bitter experience of 1241 gave King Béla IV the authority he needed to enact the defensive strategy he had preferred at the time, so he took action to capitalize on the three factors of strength that had been helpful against the Mongols: the employment of foreign knights including the religious orders, the Danube barrier and the need for stone fortresses. Beginning with the army, Béla amalgamated the *servientes regales* and the *iobagiones castri* into a new class of heavily armoured and well-trained knights of the western type as castellans or armed retainers. This brought a new unity between aristocrats and lesser fighting men and improved the latter's material conditions. In 1267 Béla conferred upon both groups the status of *nobiles* (nobility), previously reserved only for aristocrats, thus creating a single noble class encompassing all free fighting men (Ertman 1997: 273–74). Foreign help was nevertheless eagerly sought, and on 2 June 1247 Béla entered into a new contract with the Knights Hospitaller who had served him so well in 1242. He placed them in key strategic positions and required them to engage in castle-building because his own people were not sufficiently skilled or experienced in it. He also obliged the Hospitallers to fortify and repopulate Transylvania, while also providing 60 knights against the Mongol threat and 50 knights to garrison castles in the west against any potential Christian foes (Pow 2019a: 243). One key position was the Turnu Roşu Pass that had been used as a point of access by the Mongols in the first invasion. Consideration was also given to weapons, and in 1259 Béla wrote to Pope Alexander IV asking for 1,000 crossbowmen to be sent (Szőcs 2010: 18).

Béla also took great pains to speed up the Kingdom of Hungary's fortification programme and the fortress line's important links to the Danube. In a letter sent to Pope Innocent IV on 11 November 1247 Béla insisted that it was in the best interests of the whole of Europe that the river should be reinforced with castles. To Béla the key was always the Danube, with a stout ten-month campaign of resistance despite the fact that the country lacked fortresses and the troops to man them (Sălăgean 2016: 60). With these words Béla set out to construct a new diplomatic doctrine of a frontier ideology, based upon the concept of Hungary as the bulwark of Christendom in both a symbolic and a practical sense.

In this Béla was effectively starting from Ground Zero, because hardly any town in the Kingdom of Hungary had been able to protect its inhabitants during the 1241 invasion. Only six castles out of 29 in the Mongol-occupied part of the country had held out against their attacks, all but one of which were built on elevated sites. Fügedi (1986: 47) quotes a 19th-century historian's description of the fortresses as earth or mud pies that used to be called castles. Nevertheless, whatever their weaknesses, the presence of castles and the consequent need for siege warfare had neutralized, or at the very least hampered, two of the Mongols' most valuable assets: their speed of advance and their mobility. Esztergom had been a good example that contrasted with the experiences of the central Balkans, which was a region too poor to afford substantial fortifications and ended up being occupied by the Mongols (Sedlar 1994: 117). At the opposite extreme the Mongols left the Byzantine Empire well alone, hence the comment by the Emperor of Nicaea John III Vatatzes (r. 1222–54), who sent emissaries to the Mongols but thought little of them once he had come to know them (MFW: 187).

The new fortification strategy for Hungary meant that old castles had to be rebuilt and new ones added; a task in which Béla encouraged his great lords to play their part, although this may have been ordered somewhat reluctantly because the Hungarian crown did not have the resources to finance the rebuilding of all the sites in stone. Béla was therefore forced

to license private individuals and institutions to build fortifications, a step that all previous monarchs had tried to avoid. In delivery terms the process would be a success, because of the 63 new or rebuilt castles whose ownership is known, 30 were in private hands, built and garrisoned mainly by leading aristocrats and churchmen. After the death of King Béla IV in 1270, 88 of the 110 new castles for the period 1270–1300 were privately owned (Fügedi 1986: 50–62).

The operations included the building of a fortress at Buda opposite Pest, and Visegrád provides another good example of the underlying process. The exact stages of its rebuilding are unclear, but a charter of 1251 indicates that a functioning royal residence was already in existence and it is also recorded that in 1259 the king gave the castle to his wife. The new fortress had an upper citadel surrounded by stone walls with towers and a drawbridge, while the lower castle's defences included the Solomon Tower, a large, hexagonal residential tower dating from the late 13th century. The site would be defended successfully during a civil war in 1284 (Pow 2019a: 244). Elsewhere we are told that the bishop of Vác rented a stone tower in 1285 to ensure the safety of his dependants in case of an attack by Cumans among others (Berend 2001: 46). The value of stout fortresses had clearly been accepted.

In conclusion, an earlier generation of historians have tended to regard the Mongols as invincible. Such impressions have sometimes been drawn from accounts written by scribes who had become servants of the Mongols and were eager to please their masters, but the propaganda arm of the Mongol conquerors had always been ready to supply tales of terror and inevitable victory. It is beyond the scope of this book to consider the very real defeats that were heaped upon other Mongol armies by the Mamluks

When the Mongols left Croatia King Béla IV returned to Hungary to see for himself the devastation that the Mongols had caused. A depleted population meant that fields could not be tilled, and an epidemic in 1243 led to a serious famine that probably claimed more victims than the invasion.

The stark modern memorial to the battle of Muhi. It probably marks the spot where the Hungarian army set up their defended camp. The land is flat all around, including the area where most of the fighting probably took place.

of Egypt at Ayn Jālūt on 3 September 1260, or by the samurai of Japan during a seaborne invasion in November 1274, other than to say that the Mamluks outwitted the Mongols by luring them into an ideal battlefield. They then took advantage of their own skills at archery and the intelligence supplied by an informer, and destroyed the Mongol army by means of a tactical envelopment.

Even if we confine ourselves just to the two bodies of troops discussed here – the Hungarian army and the Polish knights, both of whom were backed up by chivalric visitors from Western Europe – the Mongols were clearly not invincible. All in all, the Mongol invasion of Hungary in 1241–42 was a brief historical episode in which the nobility, clergy and population of the country suffered an enormous shock. They encountered a little-known and poorly understood enemy who were not a raiding band of steppe horsemen but a well-organized large army attacking the country with the intention to subjugate or destroy the population, and somehow they had survived.

Finally, deep within the overwhelmingly grim and negative analysis of the Mongol invasion of Eastern Europe there lay an unexpected positive strand, because many years earlier certain rumours about the first Mongol advances had identified them with legendary Christian forces located somewhere in the East which, it was assumed, might even be recruited for crusading purposes against Islam. Following the invasion of Hungary Pope Innocent IV sent no fewer than three embassies to the Mongols as part of this optimistic aspiration. The most celebrated of the missions took place in 1245 and was led by John of Plano Carpini who was quoted earlier on military matters, but other reports he sent back to Rome were not what the Pope wished to hear. Instead of enthusing about the recruitment of potential crusaders John passed on the Mongols' supposed intentions to bring the whole world into subjection. It may have been bluff, but John was told that two armies had already been despatched for a fresh assault upon Poland and Hungary, while future Mongol invasion plans included the Baltic states of Livonia, Prussia and even Italy itself (HM: 80).

Aftermath

Both Poland and Hungary would suffer renewed Mongol invasions by the Golden Horde, and the events that took place during those later years enable us to assess the effectiveness of the precautions King Béla IV had put in place since 1242. Poland was attacked anew in 1259 by Batu's brother Berke. There was a fresh assault on Łuck, after which Sandomierz experienced a four-day siege. An army under the Mongol general Boroldai devastated the city along with Kraków and, in the opinion of one Polish chronicler, the invasion of 1259 exceeded the 1241 campaign in its ferocity (Jackson 2005: 123). After the fresh disaster stone walls would be added to both places, so that by 1289 Kraków would boast strong stone fortifications supported by catapults and both large and small revolving crossbows, which implies ones that were wall-mounted on a swivel (GVC: 116).

In December 1259 the Mongols enclosed Sandomierz with a stockade and bombarded the walls with catapults under the cover of a steady fire of arrows. When the ramparts were destroyed they placed scaling ladders against the rubble and climbed over into the town (GVC: 79). The Dominicans of St Jacob's church suffered a savage massacre of 49 of their number that is solemnly commemorated in the city today, while in Kraków the Mongol incursion is remembered more colourfully. The first means is the famous trumpet call played from the tower of the Mariacki (St Mary's) church, based on the popular Polish legend of the trumpeter of Kraków playing the *hejnał mariacki* (St Mary's Trumpet Call), and being shot through the throat by an arrow after only a few notes. The other is the Lajkonik festival during which a rider in Mongol costume tours the streets on a hobby horse collecting a symbolic ransom and touching spectators with his mace for good luck.

Hungary was attacked anew when an army from the Golden Horde invaded during the winter of 1285/86, but this second Mongol invasion of Hungary had a very different outcome from the first. The incursion was

probably not conducted on the scale of the 1241 operation because the Golden Horde were far more interested in fighting in north-west Persia and the Caucasus than in Europe. Their direction of advance is not known for certain but was probably through Transylvania. The initial invasion was steady and successful and they ravaged Pest, yet once again they were stopped by the Danube and hindered by the new stone fortifications within which the Hungarian inhabitants took refuge; but the big difference from 1241 was that there was no battle of Muhi. King László (Ladislaus) IV (r. 1272–90), the grandson of King Béla IV, marshalled his field armies far more effectively than his grandfather had done, avoiding confrontations on open plains, denying the invaders supplies through a scorched-earth policy and seeking combat only among the hills. He was also helped by the weather, because the winter of 1285/86 was very different from the severe frost of 1242, and when the Mongols began their withdrawal they were impeded by heavy rain, snow and swollen rivers that turned the plains of Hungary into a vast morass and drowned many in the floods. The Mongols made a fighting retreat through Transylvania and destroyed several weakly defended points, but snow and ice slowed their pace, leaving them prey to raiding, and according to some sources they were also misled by their Russian guides (Szőcs 2010: 21–24).

Most significantly of all the Golden Horde lost a fierce battle at the castle of Torockó (Rimetea) in Transylvania, where 1,000 Mongols were taken prisoner. The defeat of the invaders showed just how much had changed, because their predecessors had destroyed the former wooden fortress in 1241; by 1285 it had been rebuilt in stone and withstood the fresh assault (Szőcs 2010: 27). Great hunger then set in so that the Mongols may even have resorted to cannibalism of their captives. They certainly suffered heavy losses and at the end their leader escaped on foot with his wife and his mare as all he had left (GVC: 96). It was an ignominious withdrawal, and such was the shift in the balance of power that towards the end of his reign King László IV was able to take some

Mongol contingents into his service. Apart from sporadic raiding the Golden Horde gave Hungary few worries in the years to come, and in 1345, just over 100 years after Muhi, a knight called András Lackfi led a Hungarian army to victory over the Mongols in Moldavia. By this time political disintegration and rivalry within the Golden Horde had taken their toll, and the episode in the history of the Mongols that had involved the battles of Liegnitz and Muhi would forever mark their giant empire's westward limit.

The castle of Boldogkő in northern Hungary was one of many fortresses rebuilt after the Mongol invasion of 1241/42. It stands on a curious natural rock formation like the prow of a ship.

The castle of Torockó in Transylvania withstood a Mongol attack in 1285 and 1,000 Mongols were taken prisoner. Their predecessors had destroyed the former wooden fortress in 1241; by 1285 it had been rebuilt in stone and stood up to the fresh assault. (Einstein2/ Wikimedia/CC BY-SA 3.0)

BIBLIOGRAPHY

A note on sources

The primary sources for the Mongol campaign against Eastern Europe are written either in Latin or in Chinese. Fortunately, all of them have been translated into English within the past 20 years in one form or another, so an author is able to gain a much better view of the progress of the operation than was formerly available. The Hungarian accounts are a mixture of first-hand observation and material drawn in all probability from participants in the fighting. The devastation they record is quite moving, and has been corroborated by modern archaeological investigation. The Chinese account is also remarkable for its frank claims that the Mongols were worried about losing the battle of Muhi at a crucial stage in the conflict.

The main source for the battle of Liegnitz and the Polish campaign is *The Annals of Jan Długosz* (AJD). It is far from being an eyewitness account as it was composed by Jan Długosz two centuries later, but most probably Długosz used sources that have since been lost. The primary sources for the battle of Muhi and the Hungarian campaign are Thomas of Split's *History of the Bishops of Salona and Split* (HBS) and a shorter account in Master Roger's *Epistle to the Sorrowful Lament* (ESL), a remarkable document that includes his personal account of the experience of being a captive of the Mongols. The battle of Muhi is also the only medieval encounter fought on European soil for which we have a descriptive account in Chinese, namely Sübe'etei's biography in *Yuan shi* (YS) of which three versions exist. *The Galician-Volynian Chronicle* (GVC) and *The Chronicle of Novgorod* (CN) provide fascinating details about contemporary Mongol warfare in other theatres. Finally, we have the reports brought back by three key envoys sent to the Mongols: John of Plano Carpini (HM), William of Rubruck (MFW) and the *Tartar Relation* (TR). Any other material from primary sources is referenced according to the compiler or translator.

Primary sources in English translation

AJD: *The Annals of Jan Długosz*. Allan, Jane, Maurice, Michael & Smith, Paul (1997). *The Annals of Jan Długosz: A History of Eastern Europe from A.D. 965 to A.D. 1480: An English Abridgement*. London: IM Publications.

CN: *The Chronicle of Novgorod*. Michell, Robert & Forbes, Nevill (trans.) (1914). *The Chronicle of Novgorod, 1016–1471*. London: Camden Society.

ESL: *Epistle to the Sorrowful Lament upon the Destruction of the Kingdom of Hungary by the Tatars*. Bak, János M., Rady, Martin C. & Veszpremy, Laszlo (trans.) (2010). *Anonymous and Master Roger: The Deeds of the Hungarians. Epistle to the Sorrowful Lament upon the Destruction of the Kingdom of Hungary by the Tatars*. Budapest: Central European University.

GVC: *The Galician-Volynian Chronicle*. Perfecky, George (trans.) (1973). *The Hypatian Codex, Part II: The Galician-Volynian Chronicle*. Harvard Series in Ukrainian Studies 16:2. Munich: Wilhelm Fink Verlag.

HBS: *History of the Bishops of Salona and Split*. Karbić, Damir, Matijević-Sokol, Mirjana & Sweeney, James Ross (trans. & eds) (2006). *Archdeacon Thomas of Split, Historia Salonitanorum atque Spalatinorum pontificum / History of the bishops of Salona and Split*. (Latin text by Olga Perić.) Budapest: Central European University Press.

HM: *The story of the Mongols whom we call the Tartars*. Hildinger, Erik (trans.) (2003). *Historia Mongalorum quos nos Tartaros appellamus : Friar Giovanni di Plano Carpini's account of his embassy to the court of the Mongol Khan*. Boston, MA: Branden Books (Kindle Edition).

MFW: *The Mission of Friar William of Rubruck*. Jackson, Peter (trans.) & Morgan, David (2009). *The Mission of Friar William of Rubruck: His Journey to the Court of the great Khan Möngke, 1253–1255*. London: Hackett.

TR: *Tartar Relation*. Skelton, R.A., Marston, Thomas E. & Painter, George D. (1995). *The Vinland Map and the Tartar Relation*. New Haven, CT: Yale University Press.

YS: *Yuan Shi*. Pow, Stephen & Liao, Jingjing (2018). 'Subutai: Sorting Fact from Fiction Surrounding the Mongol Empire's Greatest General (With Translations of Subutai's Two Biographies in the *Yuan Shi*)', *Journal of Chinese Military History* 7: 37–76.

Secondary sources

Berend, Nora (2001). 'At the Gate of Christendom: Jews, Muslims and "Pagans"', in *Medieval Hungary, c.1000 – c.1300*. Cambridge: Cambridge University Press.

Burzyński, Edmund (2012). 'Templariusze w walce z najazdem Mongolskim na Polskę w 1241 roku', *Słupskie Studia Historyczne* 18: 37–60.

Dimnik, Martin (2003). *The Dynasty of Chernigov, 1146–1246*. Cambridge: Cambridge University Press.

Ertman, Thomas (1997). *Birth of the Leviathan: Building States and Regimes in Medieval and Early Modern Europe*. New York, NY: Cambridge University Press.

Fügedi, Erik (1986). *Castle and Society in Medieval Hungary (1000–1437)*. Budapest: Akadémiai Kiadó.

Giles, J.A. (1889). *Matthew Paris's English History Vol. 1*. London: Bell.

Gyucha, Attila, Lee, Wayne E. & Rózsa, Zoltán (2019). 'The Mongol Campaign in Hungary, 1241–1242: The Archaeology and History of Nomadic Conquest and Massacre', *Journal of Military History* 83: 1021–66.

Hunyadi, Zsolt (2004). 'Hospitallers in the Medieval Kingdom of Hungary c.1150–1387'. PhD dissertation. Budapest: Central European University.

Jackson, Peter (2005). *The Mongols and the West*. Harlow: Pearson.

Laszlovszky, József, Pow, Stephen & Pusztai, Tamás (2016). 'Reconstructing the Battle of Muhi and the Mongol invasion of Hungary in 1241: New Archaeological and Historical Approaches', *Hungarian Archaeology*, Winter 2016: 29–38.

Laszlovszky, József, Pow, Stephen, Romhányi, Beatrix F., Ferenczi, László & Pinke, Zsolt (2018). 'Contextualising the Mongol Invasion of Hungary in 1241–42: Short- and Long-Term Perspectives', *The Hungarian Historical Review* 7 (3): 419–50.

Luard, Henry R., ed. (1882). *Chronica Majora*. Volume VI. London: Trübner & Co.

Nicolle, D. & Shpakovsky, V. (2001). *Kalka River 1223: Genghiz Khan's Mongols invade Russia*. Campaign 98. Oxford: Osprey.

Pow, Stephen (2011). 'Deep Ditches and Well-built Walls: A Reappraisal of the Mongol Withdrawal from Europe in 1242'. MA thesis. University of Alberta, Calgary.

Pow, Stephen (2019a). 'Hungary's castle defense strategy in the aftermath of the Mongol invasion (1241–1242)', in Tkalčec, Tatjana *et al.*, *Fortifications, Defence Systems, Structures and Features in the Past*. Zagreb: Institute of Archaeology: pp. 239–50.

Pow, Stephen (2019b). 'Climatic and Environmental Limiting Factors in the Mongol Empire's Westward Expansion: Exploring causes for the Mongol withdrawal from Hungary in 1242', in Yang, Liang Emlyn *et al.*, eds, *Socio-Environmental Dynamics along the historical Silk Road*. Kiel: Kiel University, pp. 301–21.

Pow, Stephen (2021). 'Mongol Inroads into Hungary: Investigating Some Unexplored Avenues', in Maiorov, Alexander V. & Hautala, Roman, *Mongols and Central-Eastern Europe: Political, Economic, and Cultural Relations*. London: Routledge: pp. 98–118.

Pow, Stephen & Laszlovszky, József (2019). 'Finding Batu's Hill at Muhi: Liminality between Rebellious Territory and Submissive Territory, Earth and Heaven for a Mongol Prince on the Eve of Battle', *Hungarian Historical Review* 8 (2): 261–89.

Sălăgean, Tudor (2016). *Transylvania in the Second Half of the Thirteenth Century*. Leiden: Brill.

Sedlar, Jean (1994). *East Central Europe in the Middle Ages, 1000–1500*. Seattle, WA: University of Washington Press.

Sinor, Denis (1999). 'The Mongols in the West', *Journal of Asian History* 33.1: 1–44.

Spuler, Bertold (1971). *The Mongols in History*. London: Pall Mall Press.

Świętosławski, Witold (1999). *Arms and Armour of the Nomads of the Great Steppe in the times of the Mongol expansion (12th–14th centuries)*. Łódź: Oficyna Naukowa.

Szőcs, Tibor (2010). 'Egy második "tatárjárás"? A tatár–magyar kapcsolatok a XIII. század második felében (A Second Tartar Invasion? The Tartar–Hungarian Relations in the Second Half of the 13th Century)'. Belvedere 22 (3–4): 16–49.

Turnbull, Stephen (2009). 'Crossbows or Catapults? The Identification of Siege Weaponry and Techniques in the Chronicle of Henry of Livonia', in Murray, Alan V., ed., *The Clash of Cultures on the Medieval Baltic Frontier*. Farnham: Ashgate Press, pp. 307–19.

Waterson, James (2013). *Defending Heaven: China's Mongol Wars 1209–1370*. London: Frontline Books.

INDEX

References to illustrations are shown in **bold**. References to plates are shown in bold with caption pages in brackets, e.g. **38–39**, (40).

Andrew II, King of Hungary 15, 52
archers/horse-archers: (Eur) 15, 18, 21, 24; (Mon) **12**, **13**, 15, 18, 21–22, 26–27, 28, 37, **38–39**, (40), 47, 52, 56, **66–67**, (68)
armour: (Eur) 7, **11**, **15**, **16**, **17**, 20, **21**, 25, **31**, **38–39**, (40), **42**, **43**, 50, **66–67**, (68); (Mon) 5, **14**, 21, **26**, **29**, **42**, **44**, **66–67**, (68)
Austria 8, 44–45, 57, 60

Ba'atur (Mongol chief general) 54, 55, 58
Baidar (nephew of Batu) 18, 32
banners/standards: (Eur) 25, **38–39**, (40); (Mon) 26, **38–39**, (40), 41
Batu Khan (son of Jochi) 8, 18, 31, 32, 42, **47**, 48, 51, 52, 53, 68, 69, 75
Béla IV, King of Hungary 8, 15, **47**, 65, 75, 76
    at battle of Muhi **16**, **17**, 47, 48, 51, 52, 53, 54, 62: flight/pursuit of 8, 48, 57, 58, 59, 60, 69–70
    defensive strategy for Hungary 8, 46, 60, 71–73, 76
    help for the Cumans 15, 18, 31, 32, 46, 53
    return to Hungary 71, 73
Bohemia/Bohemian knights 45
Boldogko castle 77, **77**
Bolesław Dypoldowic 'the Lisper' 35, 36, 37
Bolesław V 'the Chaste' 15, **15**
Boroldai (Mongol general) 75
bows/arrows: (Eur) 7, 20–21, 24, 58; (Mon) 5, **12**, **13**, 18, 20, 22, 24, 27, **27**, 37, **38–39**, (40), 47, **47**, 52, 55, 58, 62, 64, 70, 75

cavalry forces 68
    heavy (Mon) **5**, 12, 22–23, **26**, 27, 42, **66–67**, (68)
    light: (Eur) 15, 21; (Mon) 21–22, 28, **38–39**, (40), 47, 56
Cegléd-Madarászhalom, destruction of 65
Chinggis Khan 4, 5, 6, 11, 18, 47, 53
Chmielnik, fighting at 8, 32–33, **32**, 42, 37
Croatia, Mongol actions in 7, 8, 48, 69–70, 73
crossbowmen: (Eur) 21, 24, 28, 36, 37, 59, 60, 63, **66–67**, (68); (Mon) 72
crossbows: (Eur) 20, 21, 24, **29**, 58, 59, **66–67**, (68), 75; (Mon) 64
Cumans (the) 5, 15, 18, 31, 32, 46, 53, 73

Esztergom, siege of 6, 7, 8, 20, 29–30, 57–60, **60**, 61, **61**, 62–64, 70, 71, 72

Frederick II, Duke of Austria 44–45, 57, 58

Galicia 15, 23, 53, 71
Georgia, Mongol actions in 5, 6
Géza II, King of Hungary 15
Golden Horde (the) 8, 23, 25, 53, 68, 71, 75–77
Gregory, Bishop of Győr 56
Győr, fall of 56, 64

headwear: (Eur) **15**, **16**, **17**, 20, 24–25, 37, **38–39**, (40), **42**, **43**, **66–67**, (68); (Mon) 5, 7, **12**, **13**, **19**, 22, 23, **23**, 27, 29, 30, **38–39**, (40), **42**, **44**, **66–67**, (68), 70, 76
Henry II 'the Pious', Duke 6, 7, 26, **29**, 31, 33, 41, **45**
    at Liegnitz 15, 34, 36, 37, **38–39**, (40), 41–42, **42**, 43, 44, 44
horse equipment/trappings (Eur) **16**, **17**, 23, **24**, 25; (Mon) **12**, **13**, 22, **44**

Hungarian armies/knights 8, 10, 11, 14–15, **16**, **17**, 20, 21, 47, 52, 53–54
    castellans (armed retainers) 72
    clothing/attire **11**, **16**, **17**
    'Cousins of Wahlstatt' 37, **38–39**, (40)
    iobagiones castri (castle soldiers) 11, 71
    nobiles (nobility) 72
    servientes regales (free royal knights) 11, 71
Hungary, Kingdom of
    first Mongol invasion 6, 8, **9**, 31–32, 44, 46, 47, 53, 62–65, 71, 72, **73**, 74: points of entry **9**, 45, 72; withdrawal from 8, 68–69, 76
    second Mongol invasion 8, 53, 71, 74, 75–77: defensive strategy 8, 46–47, 59, 60, 62, 68, 71, 72–73, 76

Iwanowic, Jan 42–43

Jebe (Mongol general) 5
Jochi (son of Chinggis Khan) 47, 53

Kalka River, battle of the (1223) 5, 6
Kálmán, King of Galicia 15, 53, 54, 57, **58**
Klis castle, Mongol attack on 57, 59, 69, **69**, 70
Knights Hospitaller of St John 10, 20, 64, **66–67**, (68), 69, 72
Knights Templar 10, 20, 33, 36, **37**, 54, 64
Kozel'sk, fall of 53, 60
Kraków, fall of 8, **28**, 32, 33, 60, 75
Kyiv, fall of 8, 31, 64

lances: (Eur) 11, **16**, **17**, 24, 25, **42**, (Mon) **38–39**, (40), 42
László IV, King of Hungary 76–77
Legnickie Pole 34, **35**, 36, 41
Liegnitz, battle of 6, 7, 8, 10, 15, 16, 19, 20, **29**, 31–34, **35**, 41–45, **42**, **44**, 53, 59, 64, 77
    battlefield, features of **34**, **37**, **41**
    dispositions/tactics 36–37, **38–39**, (40), 41
    losses 37, 41, 42, 43
Lublin, fall of 8, 32
Łuck, Mongol attacks on 30, 75

maces: (Eur) 18, 25, 64; (Mon) 22, 28, 23, 64, 65, **66–67**, (68)
Matthias, Archbishop of Esztergom 56
mercenaries: (Eur) 36; (Mon) 10, 18
    Venetian *ballistarii*/crossbowmen 59
Mieszko II 'the Fat', Duke 15, 33, 34, 36, 37
Mongol armies/warriors
    clothing **12**, **13**, **19**, 21–22, 23, **27**, 30, 76
    composition/size of 11, 14, 18
    formations/tactics 25, 26: envelopment/ encirclement 25, 26, 37; escape route (enemy forces) 28, 55–56; fast charge 18–19; feigned retreat 8, 21, 24, 25–26, 32, 34, 50–51; forlorn-hope squads 18, 29–30, 69, 70; ghost riders 26; mêlée actions 28; skirmishers/skirmishing 26; smokescreens **38–39**, (40), 41
    imagery/perception of 4, 7, 14, **59**, 73–74
    social hierarchy/'nobility' 11
Mongolia 5, 8, 19, 20, 56, 68–69
Montenegro, Mongol actions in 70
Moravia, Mongol forces in 8, 42, 45
Muhi, battle of 8, 10, **12**, **13**, 14, 15, **16**, **17**, 18, 20, 27, 45, 46–48, 50–56, **52**, 57, 64, 76, 77
    battlefield, features of 47, 48, **51**, **56**, 74, **74**
    forces' dispositions/tactics 26, 28, 48, **49**, 50–51, 55–56
    losses 52, 54, 56

Ögedei Khan 6, 53, 68, 69, **70**
Oleśnica Mała, destruction of 33, 36
Opole-Racibórz 15, 36
Orda (brother of Batu) 18, 32, 53
Orosháza-Bónum, destruction of 65

Pest, fall of 8, 47, 50, 52, 57, 58, 59, 60, **61**, 62, 65, 73, 76
Poland, Mongol actions in 8, 32–33, 36, 44–45, 71, 74, **76**
Polish army/knights 8, 32–33, 36, 37, 41, 42–43, 74
    composition 10, 15
    first Mongol invasion 6, 8, 15, 18, 75
    second Mongol invasion 8, 10–11, 53, 75

Qaidan (brother of Batu) 8, 32

Rothkirch (standard bearer) 37, **38–39**, (40)
Ruś/Russia, Mongol actions in 4–5, 6, 7, 8, 29, 31, 47, 53, 60, 68
Ruś/Russian armies 5, 25
Ryazan, fall of 7, 29, 31

Sandomierz, fall of 8, 10–11, 15, 23, **30**, 32, **32**, 42, 75, **76**
Serbia, Mongol forces in 70, 71
shields (Eur) 7, 11, **15**, **16**, 20, 24, 25, **31**, 37, **38–39**, (40), **66–67**, (68); (Mon) 5, 22, 28, **66–67**, (68)
siege engines/equipment: (Eur) 64, 69; (Mon) 28, 29, 59, 62, 70
    battering rams (Mon) 29, 31, 60
    catapults: (Eur) 58; (Mon) 28, 29, 30, 31, 48, 54, 55, 59, 60, 62, **65**, 75
    scaling ladders (Mon) 29, 75
    traction trebuchets 29, 30
siege warfare (Mon) 6, 28–30, 65, 72
Silesia 10, 15, 32, 33, 44
Silesian knights/nobles 36, 37, **38–39**, (40)
spears: (Eur) 11, **21**, 64; (Mon) 22, 23, 28, 42, 56, 64, 70
Split 20, 59, 69
Sübe'etei (Mongol general) 5, 8, 18, **27**, 36–37, 53, 54, 64
swords: (Eur) **16**, 20, 21, 25, **38–39**, (40), **43**, 50, 64, **66–67**, (68); (Mon) **13**, 22, 23, **27**, 28, **30**, 47, 56, 64, **66–67**, (68)
Székesfehérvár, siege of 7, 20, 60, **61**, 63, 64–65, **66–67**, (68), 70

Torockó castle, attack on 76–77, **77**
Torzhok, fall of 31, 60
Transylvania 8, 53, 68–69, 72, 76, 77

Ugrin, Archbishop of Kalocsa 47, 50, **50**, 52, 53, 54, 56
Ukraine, Mongol actions in 8, 30, 31, 53

Veszprém, protection of 64
Visegrád fortress **61**, 64, 73, **76**
Vladimir, fall of 7, 31
Voczon, Master Rembald de 54
Volodymyr-Volynskyi, burning of 8, 32

Wenceslaus I, King of Bohemia 36, 45
Wrocław 8, 34, 36, 37, 44
    fall of 32, 33, **33**, 60

Zawichost, fall of 8, 32